BOTH SIDES OF THE VEIL

A Personal Experience

BY

ANNE MANNING ROBBINS

1909

TO

AUGUSTUS PEARL MARTIN

WHOSE LIFE ON EARTH EXEMPLIFIED TO THE AUTHOR, DURING AN ASSOCIATION OF EIGHT SHORT YEARS, MANY NOBLE AND BEAUTIFUL QUALITIES OF SOUL, AND WHOSE SEEMING CONTINUED EXISTENCE ON THE OTHER SIDE OF THE VEIL HAS INSPIRED NEW FAITH IN THE REALITY OF THAT OTHER LIFE,

THIS BOOK IS REVERENTLY DEDICATED

The following letter from Professor William James was addressed to the publishers:

The manuscript which this accompanies, and which I recommend hereby to your attention, is from a companion of mine in psychical research, who, from a state of doubt, has won through to a faith in human survival in a spiritual order which continues the visible order. It is a genuine record of moral and religious experience, profoundly earnest, and calculated, I should think, to interest and impress readers who desire to know adequately what deeper significances our life may hold in store.

Truly yours,
William James

All names and initials used in this book are genuine. In every instance deemed advisable the necessary permission has been obtained.

CONTENTS

CONTENTS

PART III

Suggestive Thoughts on the Attainment of Spirituality

INTRODUCTION

F. W. H. Myers says: "We receive life and knowledge, which it is our business to develop into Love and Wisdom and Joy."[1]

William James says: "The whole subject of immortal life has its prime roots in personal feeling. . . . There are individuals with a real passion for the matter, men and women for whom a life hereafter is a pungent craving, and the thought of it an obsession; and in whom keenness of interest has bred an insight into the relations of the subject that no one less penetrated with the mystery of it can attain. Some of these people are known to me. They are not official personages; they do not speak as the scribes, but as having direct authority. And surely, if anywhere a prophet clad in goatskins, and not a uniformed official, should be called to give inspiration, assurance, and instruction, it would seem to be here, on such a theme."[2]

The business of life as concisely stated by Myers I have been and still am endeavoring to carry on, and I find it a business which I shall wish to pursue to the day of my death, and quite possibly thereafter. I offer both quota-

[1] Human Personality and its Survival of Bodily Death. Vol. II, p. 310.

[2] Human Immortality, pp. 3, 4.

tions as justification, if justification be needed, for the publication of the present volume. My real authority, however, must be, not what others have thought and said, with all due respect for the writers quoted, and with gratitude for the expression of the ages inextricably woven into the literature of our own generation; but the authority of deep conviction, of actual experience, of ever-widening vision, of increasing happiness, of growing power, and the belief that these things are for all who will seek.

There is nothing more patent to the observer and the thinker than the differences in capacity with which men are born. Let that fact be explained as it may, or not explained at all, it has always seemed to me unreasonable to complain of the condition in which one finds one's self when awakening to consciousness in early life; for whoever will make use of his God-given faculties, whether he be a savage of the lowest type or an Eastern sage, whether he occupy a plane but little removed from the animal or have back of him ages of inherited thought, may make that degree of progress in his life between birth and the grave which shall be to *him* a satisfaction, which shall bring to *him* the good which he craves. To this end it is not necessary to understand the whole scheme of creation, or to be able to say positively that such and such things are so, but what *seems* to be true to a person who clarifies his brain and purifies his heart, and then looks and listens, is generally a safe guide for that person. In fact, it is often the person who appears to the casual observer to have no religion at all, because it cannot be expressed by or comprised in any creed or dogma, who is most likely to have a religion of his own, sincere, deep, vital and soul-saving. By many a system of philosophy and through many a religious creed the human soul has continued its search after self-knowledge and God knowledge, yet each one in his own generation must begin as a little child to find out for himself the relation between himself and his Maker, must make the knowledge his individual possession, as if no one had ever lived and talked before.

It does not appear that one is pushed on to acquire knowledge, pushed on to master the lessons of life, pushed on to reap the profit of his experience, against his will, but from the moment that the desire makes itself felt in the soul, from that moment opportunities come. It is quite plain that opportunities come to him who deserves them, to him who is ready for them, to him who is able to seize them. And what *is* opportunity, and what do we mean by the word? Analyzed, it means the appearance before our eyes of an opening in the black wall of fate about us, through which we may express ourselves, our talents, our souls in some larger way than we have hitherto done. But, the soul is its own teacher. It is not necessary for it to be here or there in order that it may learn. It may acquire knowledge *wherever* it chances to be, by revolving in the mind whatever is suggested by its particular environment, or whatever wells up from within.

Unforeseen events seem to determine for us a course in life which proves in the end far better than anything we could possibly have planned, had the choice been absolutely in our own hands. While we are free to do as we wish within certain limits, there are boundaries beyond which we cannot go. This shaping of events points to Eternal Law, to Divine Guidance, to an Over-ruling Providence, which while great enough to control the stars in their orbits also enters each individual life.

I disclaim the slightest pretence to science, yet I understand that any one who observes facts carefully and records them truthfully, whether those facts be in the physical, mental or spiritual realm of being, is adding his mite to the accumulations of science.

I have no *scheme* of philosophy to offer, but only such bits of philosophic thought as have filtered through my own brain and shown themselves effective for good in my own life.

I wish to record here only the thoughts and experiences which are and have become my own. Whatever the origin of the thoughts, whether forced out of me by the intensity of misery, or dropped into my heart by an angel, they now belong to me. It is as if I had found myself drowning; as if absolutely nothing which I could grasp were within sight or within reach; as if, realizing my danger, I had, as the only means of saving myself, suddenly disappeared from the material and become pure ether; thus finding myself able through the inherent power of my own nature to rise out of the blackness of the engulfing waves, to float above all danger, or to land, as I choose, on solid ground.

The serious author must deliberate most carefully before committing to the cold type that which cannot be unsaid or taken back. I can only offer the present volume in the spirit of the greatest humility, yet there is something within me which is insistent upon expression. This something within me has been leading me through varied phases of life, through doubt and mental darkness, through disappointment of hopes, through loss of beloved friends, and lo! life's pathway has suddenly opened upon a bright and luminous field. At a little distance ahead of me in this same bright field there appears a veil. Written across this veil is the word "Death," and while the path which I descry in advance grows more beautiful as it approaches that veil, beyond it the brightness is yet more dazzling, so that with the light on this side and the still greater light on that, the veil itself is almost transparent.

From childhood in a country town where the orthodox church gathered within its fold all young eager spirits like my own, engrafting upon them its creed and dedicating them to its service, to a present freedom of soul which for itself fits all things into the scheme of the everlasting goodness of God, which looks with admiration, wonder and reverence, but no fear, upon the mysteries of the Universe, which realizes the presence, the sympathy and the helpfulness of friends called dead, which responds to the invisible life palpitating all about and receives energy therefrom, of this pathway and this transition I would speak.

It may be said that this is the philosophy of self-development merely, and that all such philosophy is as old as the hills. So be it. I will utter my little word too. If to the psychologist my logic seem crude, and to the *littérateur* my language inadequate, my utterance will not have been in vain if haply its message meet the need of some human heart.

PART I

PERSONAL EXPERIENCE AND GROWTH OF FAITH

I

PRELIMINARY

Since the early spring of 1881 to the time of publication I have resided in the city of Boston. My interest in Spiritism and what is known as "Psychical Research" dates from about that time. My opportunities have been unusual and my experience unique in some respects, and for that reason I feel that I ought not to withhold the experience from those who are seekers in the same field with myself, or from others in whom it may awaken an interest. I heartily wish that I might give my message dissociated from myself. Considering, however, the peculiar nature of my subject, I find that my personality must be wholly sacrificed to the object for which I write. My search after spiritual truth and the material circumstances of my life have been so closely interwoven that I cannot speak of the former without touching upon the latter. In fact, it is the close association and interdependence of the material and the spiritual which I wish to make prominent in this brief narrative, and were it not for that relation I should not assume that the outward affairs of an ordinary routine life could have the slightest interest for any one.

In order to make clear the different phases in the development of my faith I shall be obliged to go back a few years previous to 1881 and speak briefly of my early religious experience.

II

MOUNT HOLYOKE AND LOSS OF A CREED

When I was sixteen years old I left home for the first time, and entered Mount Holyoke Seminary, now Mount Holyoke College. Homesick girls of sixteen, surrounded by strangers and awed by superiors, are doubtless extremely impressionable. Some aged divine from Boston was holding religious meetings at the seminary. It was impressed upon me very strongly that I ought to "be converted," but *how* to become converted puzzled my brain and my heart. I knew that is was necessary to feel a conviction of sin and contrition therefor, but try as best I might I was not able to realize the enormity of sin that I was supposed to have committed during the short sixteen-years of my childhood. However, one evening I was wrought up to the point of venturing upon a personal encounter with this ministerial personage, in a private room which seems to have been used as a sort of confessional. It had the desired effect and I "became converted."

This man told me that God had been giving me good things all my life, and he asked me what I had done for God, implying that I had done absolutely nothing and that at best I was a most ungrateful creature. This argument appealed to my sense of justice, for upon reflection I could not pick out any special thing that I had done for God, and of course justice required that I should do something in return for all that He had done for me. It gave me a working basis, and I resolved that from that moment I would "do something" for God, though just what assistance the Mighty Creator wanted of such a babe was not quite clear in my mind. However, I was swept along on a wave of enthusiasm and found myself very happy. I was happy in praying for my benighted relatives who had not been through a similar experience, and I went to my bed at night with songs of joy on my lips and in my heart. My youth, my love of study and my opportunities *may* have had something to do with this happiness and possibly would have been sufficient to account for it even though the word "religion" had not been pronounced in my hearing. I believe there was, however, a new sense of being on the right track, of conscientiously endeavoring to do right, of being in harmonious relation with the Power that I conceived as God. The great life-and-death struggle of maturer years, the desperate effort of the floundering soul to save itself, was yet to come. This period at the age of sixteen I count as one of the happiest in my life. But the religion which I then professed did not make me over. It did not remove the timidity from my nature or blot out of existence certain other temperamental and possibly inherited traits which were then beginning to torment me. This required analytical thought and brave effort. Nor on the other hand did it quench a certain fearlessness of spirit which seems to have been born in me side by side with the timidity, and for which saving grace in my make-up I have always been profoundly grateful.

During my senior year at this school Bible study was an important part of the curriculum and it required considerable time each week to master the lessons which were recited on Sundays. One Sunday the presiding teacher asked for the meaning of the words "being covered with the righteousness of Christ." No one in the large class offered an answer until I attempted one by expressing the idea that because we have no righteousness of our own we must be covered, hidden as it were, by that of Christ, in order to be saved. If I had said that we must attempt to make for ourselves a garment pure and righteous like that of Christ, I never should have regretted my words, but what I did say I have regretted many times and wished that I might have an opportunity to unsay. For the idea then in my mind was that of Christ standing garbed in ample white robe, so full that it could spread out like wings, completely hiding from the view of a wrathful God poor creatures like ourselves, garmentless or clothed in rags. My reply appeared to give satisfaction. To-day I see not only ignorance but cowardice in my words. To-day I believe not only that we *may* have righteousness of our own, but that *not until* we *do* have such righteousness can we or shall we be saved. Being righteous *is* salvation. As Christ set us the example, so must we follow, and as He was righteous, so must we be according to our light and our power.

At Mount Holyoke the discipline of the routine which demands of every one her best is an invaluable factor in the development of character. I shall never forget the impression made upon me by the teachers of my day through their spirit of consecration and lofty devotion to their chosen work. And I believe the same powerful influence is exerted there today. They grow accustomed to their work, they forget themselves, and they little realize the effect which the developed beauty of their lives makes upon the sensitive girl from the country away from home for the first time in her life, for the first time brought into contact with her peers and superiors.

The religious teaching of those years,—why speak of it? Let them praise it or criticise it who will. The true inwardness of it made it worthy, left its impress upon the pupil and gradually cast into the shadow of inconsequentiality all outward observance. To the freed mind the extreme exactions of conscientious, orthodox Christianity, fearful lest it shall not do right, seem puerile. Yet through all these different forms of religion one sees the self-same effort of the soul, the effort to comprehend its true place in the Cosmos and to find its true relation to God.

It does not seem to me necessary for a person to be told in the freshness of his youth, when he knows almost nothing about sin from any experience of his own, that a gulf lies between himself and God, that God has cast him out from His presence, that only in meek dependence upon the saving grace of another's virtue and the sacrifice of another's life may he be reinstated in the Divine favor. Is it not better to present to the young mind the beauty of goodness, the delight of conforming to righteous laws as the natural way of living? If a Christ had within him a saving grace and a righteous power, it is enough to hold up His life as an ideal, and better for the youth to follow that ideal of his own accord because it is shown to him to be altogether lovely, and not because he must fear dire punishment if he does not. Yet the thinker — and everyone *may* think — is bound to come out at last into spiritual freedom through any and every path.

The instructors in this particular college who were there in my day will always be remembered by me as among the loveliest, loftiest, noblest characters it has ever been my good fortune to know. They set before their pupils the saving truth by its daily exemplification. Though there may have been grades among them, I make no exception, for at the institution founded by Mary Lyon no one is ever called to the sacred work of teaching who has not already shown herself to be a consecrated soul.

Yet when I returned to my home I saw that my father, who was a close student of nature but passed for a skeptic in matters of religion, however much I might pray for him could no more change his nature than the leopard could change his skin. I felt there must be something wrong with my belief. I was asking God for that which was contrary to laws of His own making. My reason showed me that facts are unalterable, that the unalterableness of things is what makes them facts. My belief was a changeable thing; my belief must accommodate itself to facts, for facts would never adjust themselves to it.

And my oldest sister was a lovely person. She was lovely to look at, kind and gentle in her actions; her sweet voice and her musical talent made beautiful music in the home; she was a second mother to us all. Why, then, should I wish to change her nature? Her nature was in my opinion quite adorable. Yet she somehow seemed to lack a religious creed of which I could approve. She believed if we do well here we shall do well hereafter, but she had no elaborate scheme of salvation such as had been drilled into me; an angry God, an incarnation, a sacrifice, an atonement, and the hiding behind His garments. Again my philosophy must somehow be changed so as to include this motherly girl, for I could not possibly believe that a good God would condemn her. This beloved sister passed out of the body in 1881.

My mother always has been and is to-day in her extreme old age devoted to her church and her creed, yet her charity has been of the broadest kind and she was never coercive in matters of religion. Blessed be mothers like mine.

In a very short time after leaving college I felt my religious creed slipping from me. I could not hold it. It did not satisfy my requirements. As is usual, I believe, with devotees who cut loose from the bonds of their early faith, I swung to the other extreme and clung to no dogma at all. For a brief period I experienced a sort of exultant, reckless joy in my newly acquired independence. It was delightful to think that I was not bound to accept as authoritative any religious creed or any code of philosophy laid down in any book. I was, after all, arbiter of my own fate. I could do as I pleased so long as I did not positively injure others. I might be a creature that was to live for all eternity for aught I knew. I knew nothing about it. But, I reasoned, if this be so, there is time enough for learning one's lessons. I shall reach my destination in time or eternity, and if I dilly-dally a little on the way it only hinders my own progress and harms no one else. Was this all? No. There made itself heard within me a voice which said: "To refrain from injury to your neighbor is not enough. You must do no harm to yourself. You are bound to your fellow creatures. Any injury to yourself will necessarily be felt by them. *You must preserve inviolate the purity of your own nature. You must seek knowledge and you must diffuse light.*"

Yet I was a creature of moods, now happy, now the reverse, altogether subject to them, and suffering much from self-condemnation. I do not, however, claim a monopoly in suffering, nor do I propose to discuss these uninteresting things here, further than to say that as soon as I found that I need not be slave, but might be master, of both physical sensation and mental mood, I began to make some headway, and I believe it was the reading of Plato that first gave me an insight into this important truth.

III

MEANS OF LIVELIHOOD

I had a great desire to live in a large city where I might come in contact with all phases of life and take advantage of the opportunities which such a centre affords. After leaving school I resided a short time in Philadelphia, where I practically began the battle of life. From the time I set foot in Boston, in 1881, my hands and my mind have been fully occupied, and the gaining of a sufficient livelihood has been a comparatively easy matter.

I was engaged from the very first in stenographic and clerical work, mostly stenographic. For a few years I occupied a position in the office of a commercial firm. From 1885 to 1899 I served as official stenographer in the office of what was then the Board of Police of the city of Boston, reporting hearings, conferences, conversations, and during the last five years of that period acting as private secretary to the chairman of the board. From 1900 to 1902 I was private secretary to the Water Commissioner of the city, whose office was at City Hall. From 1903 to the present time, 1909, I have been engaged in the office of a Bureau of the Massachusetts State Board of Agriculture. These several periods stand out clearly in my own mind, and reference to them may have to be made in the following chapters.

In addition to this regular occupation I had other work which occupied much of my spare time, it being mostly, however, of the same nature as my daily work. In Philadelphia I had studied a system of shorthand-writing which was then new, a system which its author claimed was equal to any of the older systems in its adaptability and yet was much more easily acquired. Soon after reaching Boston I was asked to teach the system, and from that time on, for the next ten or twelve years, I had all the private pupils I could well attend to, teaching both by correspondence and by personal lessons. I was obliged finally to drop this on account of the increasing pressure of other work.

The civil service law of Massachusetts was enacted in 1884. The rules went into effect early in 1885 and were thereafter applied as rapidly as possible to the various departments of public service. Henry Sherwin, who has been Chief Examiner for the civil service from 1884 to the present day, was just beginning to gather around him a corps of assistants in his special work of examination, a work which has grown enormously since its initiation. Soon after my own examination I was appointed one of the examiners, having been a member of one board continuously from that time to this, and serving from 1902 to

1907, inclusive, as a member of two other boards.

As I look back I can see many events which apparently *happened*, yet it seems to me now that nothing really ever happens. That is our word for something which seems to come by chance, but which may in reality have been a long time in preparing. If one has a purpose in life, or a serious intent, the person and the event are somehow brought together when the time is ripe for the accomplishment of the purpose or the furthering of the intent.

For instance, when I began teaching shorthand my system was not perfected; the author was making improvements in it, and I did not feel that I had it sufficiently at my command to undertake the teaching of it. Yet I was afraid to let the opportunity slip. I had a dim notion, even then, of unused organs becoming atrophied, and of lost opportunities blocking the appearance of others. I looked at life in its youth as a narrow stream of water running between high banks. So long as the stream does not swell, gains no accretions, it cannot branch off into other channels or flow out into meadow lakes. And so I accepted the task, my pupils agreeing to follow me in any changes which might be introduced, and the system was thereafter gradually perfected.

About this time it happened that William H. Lee, who for many years filled the position of Clerk of Committees for the City Government, wanted to know something about the new system of shorthand and engaged me to teach it to him. It happened, again, that in the year 1885 the charter of the city of Boston was amended by the legislature of Massachusetts, and, among other changes made, the control of the large police force of the city was taken from the mayor and city council and put into the hands of a commission of three, who were appointed by the Governor of the Commonwealth, to whom they were answerable for the proper management of the force. Mr. Lee was appointed one of the members of this first Metropolitan Board of Police, serving for nine years. When he took office, in 1885, he was broad-minded enough to see that the position of reporter for the board could, not improperly, be filled by a woman, in which opinion his fellow-members of the board coincided. At that time there were comparatively few women occupying positions as official stenographers or court reporters, though there are many such today.

There was apparently very little significance attaching to the question of whether I should or should not do a little teaching, whether I wished or did not wish to spend my time in that way, but if I had not undertaken it at just the time that I did, I should never have been drawn into the particular associations, or into the particular stream of events, the outcome of which seems to me of sufficient importance and interest to put upon permanent record and offer to others. That matter remains, however, for the reader to decide for himself.

My years in the police department were of the greatest benefit to me, disciplining me in many ways. The nature of the work required the concentration of all my powers in order to accomplish it with any degree of satisfaction to myself. The humanism of our common life, in aspects humorous and again interesting even to pathos, was often brought out in occurrences which took place before my eyes, and the *camaraderie* of my daily associations, deepening in some instances into the sincerity of friendship, will long be treasured in my memory.

Far be it from me to belittle any kind of work, of any grade whatever, performed in public or private capacity. The machinery of government of this great Country must be kept moving. The greater the skill and the intelligence of the thousands of men and women who stand behind the wheels, the better the government. And what is government for but to *serve* the people. Serve them how? By helping them to live healthy, normal, peaceful, progressive lives.

Yet all the while there has been with me an

undercurrent of unrest, a feeling that some one else might fill my place just as well or better than I, and a secret wish that I might do some little work in the course of my life that should be of a different grade and of more permanent value.

And why is it of any consequence to speak here of my work at all? It is simply this: since I have been trusted by city and state, my work generally approved and placed on file among public records, and since I have been accredited with sanity and a fair degree of intelligence, I ask, in all humility, that the same courtesy and confidence be extended to me when I offer records of other matters of an entirely different nature from that which is known as " red tape " of government work.

LEONORA E. PIPER
IN EARLY MARRIED LIFE

IV

EARLY ACQUAINTANCE WITH MRS. PIPER

1885

It was during the winter of 1884-5 that I became acquainted with Mrs. Leonora E. Piper, the famous psychic who for so many years has been generously contributing of her time and her special gifts to the cause of spiritual science, under the auspices of the English Society for Psychical Research. I was invited one evening with a personal friend to a family gathering of about a dozen people, because of my newly awakened interest in phenomena called psychical. Mr. Piper, senior, was present, as were also Mrs. Piper and her husband. The personality of Mrs. Piper, then a young woman, with her sweet, pure, refined and gentle countenance, attracted me at once.

The company sat around a large table, and I think there were one or two sensitives present who made some little exhibition of their powers, but nothing occurred that made any impression upon me, or that remained in my memory, outside of what was connected with Mrs. Piper. During the course of the evening she retired with one or two of her friends to a small room adjoining and opening into the large room in which the company was assembled, and, as I understood, " went under control," whatever that might mean. It was something new and strange to me. I think she had not then begun to give sittings outside of the immediate circle of her own family, but was in the process of developing her powers. Her husband explained to me that she was a little bashful about going into trance under the eyes of other people, and for that reason had retired to the smaller room. I heard the sound as of some one talking in a low tone issuing from the small room, and as I remember Mr. Piper told me that the poet Longfellow was supposed to be speaking through his wife, and a little later in the evening that " Dr. Phinuit " had arrived.

" Dr. Phinuit " was the name assumed by the early spirit-control of Mrs. Piper. He claimed to have been a French physician who passed out of the body somewhere in the vicinity of twenty-five years previous to his returning through the organism of Mrs. Piper. While under the control of Phinuit, Mrs. Piper rose and walked out into the large room, and the control addressed a few remarks to the company in general. I chanced to be standing near Mrs. Piper with the lady who was my companion that evening, and Dr. Phinuit

[Mrs. P.] put his hand on my shoulder and said in his emphatic way, addressing us both, "You are *very* harmonious."

This was my introduction to Dr. Phinuit, dear old Phinuit of those early days, for it proved in course of time that, in spite of any and all idiosyncrasies and crudities which this personality displayed, he succeeded in endearing himself to all those with whom he had numerous conversations, probably without exception, some of whom speak of him to this day with familiar affection.

I lost no time in making an appointment for a private interview with Mrs. Piper, to take place as soon as she might be ready to see me, and my notebook gives April, 1885, as the date of my first sitting. This antedates by some months Professor William James's acquaintance with her, and he is the person who introduced her, in May, 1887, to the man who became the first American Secretary of the English Society for Psychical Research. Up to the time when Professor James made her acquaintance, in the autumn of 1885, she was not known as a psychic, nor even as a person who gave promise of developing psychic gifts, except to a small number of friends and acquaintances of her immediate family.

The hour was to me one of extreme fascination. Was Dr. Phinuit really a discarnate spirit, temporarily and partially incarnated in this woman's body for the purpose of conversing with me? If so, how fortunate was I to be witness of so mysterious and interesting a phenomenon, interesting and significant wholly apart from what was said in the trance. For let it be remembered that I am not presuming to discuss the nature of the trance from the standpoint of psychology. I realize that what is said while the medium is entranced is to the psychologist all-important in his interpretation of the phenomena as such. I wish to record only observations and impressions, leaving theoretics to the scientist, to whom they properly belong. And while I may speak of my impressions *as if* they conveyed to me facts, I understand that the scientist must have something more than impressions before he can put before the world what he calls scientific truth.

I found that Dr. Phinuit understood me,—and who does not flatter himself that he is not ordinarily understood? He seemed to know all about my good points and somehow to have a special knowledge of my failings, and from that time on he sustained the relation of adviser and friend. I was altogether too proud to impart my secrets to even the closest living acquaintance, yet, confession being good for the soul, I found myself confessing freely to Phinuit. But although I may have appeared to those who knew me during this period foolishly eager to get advice from such a friend, or from any supposed spirit who professed to be able to give advice, I laid it down as a working principle, in the very earliest days of my investigations, *not* to follow the advice of any psychic which was *contrary to the dictates of my own judgment.* I do not consider that any one who has not respect enough for his own judgment to consult it and to follow it in the conduct of his material affairs, even though it may conflict at times with what purports to be advice from spirit friends, is a fit person to carry on investigations into psychical phenomena.

I did not have frequent sittings with Mrs. Piper, but I had a number each year under the Phinuit régime during a period of ten years, which extended to September, 1895, with the exception of one season when Mrs. Piper was abroad; then there was a break of several years for various reasons, Mrs. Piper not being able to give sittings all of this time on account of ill health, and in December, 1899, I had my first sitting under the latter-day régime, an account of which will be given later.

My first sitting, in April, 1885, took place about three months after the death of a friend whose acquaintance I had made when living in Philadelphia, by name Hiram Hart. [In old reports he is called "H."] Dr. Phinuit advised me to wait about eight months longer, saying that by that time I should probably hear from this friend. I waited that length of time, and I did hear from him, as it seemed, and I witnessed the interesting phenomenon of the gradual development of a new control, for in the course of a little time Hiram Hart succeeded in controlling the organism almost as well as did Phinuit himself, and during all this period of ten years he was my special communicator, though never, of course, occupying more than a portion of the time at any one sitting. [See Proc. S. P. R., Part XXXIII, pp. 289–290.]

The Phinuit régime is ancient history now in the Piper case, and I will not dwell on it here at length. A general account of these early sittings of mine was given to the S. P. R. and is included in an article entitled " Observations of Certain Phenomena of Trance " in part XXI of the Proceedings, pp. 111–114. But Hiram Hart has shown the persistent fidelity of a returning spirit, and has been, so to speak, a " friend at court " on the Other Side, keeping himself modestly in the background in these latter years because there has not been time for me to hold much communication with him, but appearing for brief moments whenever he could serve my interests in any way in my other relations, or sending to me a message of remembrance.

It has been my habit, from the very beginning, to make notes of sittings very soon after they occurred, unless I had taken full notes during the hour, which has been my invariable custom of late years, and I have notes preserved either in shorthand or transcriptions of nearly every sitting that I ever had with Mrs. Piper or any other psychic.

Mrs. Piper builded better than she knew when she elected to reside at Arlington Heights. The place is one of the loveliest of Boston's lovely suburbs. For the dweller in the city like myself, it was most restful to take a train in the morning at an hour when the tide of humanity sets toward the city, thus leaving the suburbs quiet; to ascend to the top of the "Heights" through an avenue shaded its entire length by beautiful trees; to meet Mrs. Piper's serene face; to mount still higher to an upper chamber, lock the door, watch the psychic while she seems to lose all consciousness of my presence, and then be free to commune with — whom?

V

RICHARD HODGSON AND PSYCHICAL RESEARCH

1888

I find in my notebook a memorandum to the effect that it was on Feb. 10, 1888, that I first met Richard Hodgson at the rooms of the S. P. R. at 5 Boylston place, Boston. He had come from England early the preceding year and established himself in the city, acting first as secretary of the old American Psychical Research Society, which in 1890 became the American Branch of the English Society, which latter organization he represented for the next fifteen years. I believe he was then looking up and interviewing Mrs. Piper's early sitters and I had a note of introduction to him from Mrs. Piper herself, but found her at the rooms when I called and was introduced in person by her. From that time on during the years I saw him occasionally, not frequently. I communicated with him oftener than I saw him. I at first offered service to the Society in the line of reporting, and assisted Dr. Hodgson at times during the period of my acquaintance, sometimes gratuitously and sometimes being employed by him

RICHARD HODGSON

IN HIS FIFTIETH YEAR

to make verbatim stenographic reports of sittings, or copy of records already made. I learned his methods and became familiar with the technicalities of his system of keeping records of sittings with notes thereon. Aside from the Piper work I occasionally had sittings with other psychics with whom he had not time to carry on investigations, for the purpose of enabling him to answer more intelligently the numerous inquiries that were made at the rooms of the Society, as to where to find professionals who could be recommended as having some psychical powers. I always took notes and made more or less full reports to him of such sittings, which went on file with the S. P. R.

I find that I reported a Piper sitting for him, which he could not attend and which I think was one in a series of sittings carried on by some members of the American Society at that time in existence, as early as March 6, 1888, and in May and June of the same year I attended a short series of sittings given by Mrs. Piper for the express purpose of allowing Dr. Hodgson to find out what he could in his own way about the Phinuit personality. [See Proceedings S. P. R., Part XXI, pp. 2–3 and 59.] We three met on successive Saturday evenings, Dr. Hodgson giving his time and his effort, I giving my report, and Mrs. Piper giving her services. This series was interrupted after the fifth sitting, but those five Saturday evenings were memorable, each one of three entering upon the undertaking in the happiest of moods, and each one standing by his or her part of the agreement. Dr. Hodgson asked questions and tried various harmless experiments, or what seemed to him at that time harmless, such as putting salt on the psychic's tongue when in trance, for the purpose or ascertaining whether Phinuit was conscious of it in the trance or whether Mrs. Piper was conscious of it on coming out of the trance. These experiments are not for me to discuss here. But I will say that about twelve years later, in 1900, in some correspondence with me regarding the transformations that had taken place in ourselves during those dozen years, Dr. Hodgson admitted that what he knew in 1888 about the care with which the person of the psychic should be guarded while in trance and the conditions which should precede a sitting, was mere folly compared with the knowledge he had then gained by his experience.

I remember the freshness of his enthusiasm of those early days, his intense eagerness to "find out what is on the Other Side of the Veil." He told me then that he would not allow himself to follow any profession or be engaged in any occupation for the mere sake of making money, that he would pursue only that kind of work in life in which his heart and his soul could be absorbed, with money if possible, without it if necessary.

In all probability the very first attempts at automatic writing by Mrs. Piper occurred in some of my sittings. [See Proc. S. P. R., Part XXXIII, p. 292.] The writing there referred to as having occurred on May 23, 1891, was the first I had of any length. It was by the control "Hiram Hart." Distinct messages were given and I was asked to compare the writing with his own when in life. I did compare it, being convinced myself of the appearance in it of more than one old peculiarity, which I did not think, however, were sufficiently marked to be clear to others. Dr. Hodgson also made the comparison as an expert on handwriting, and would not admit that there was any similarity worthy of mention between the two styles except in the one capital letter "H." This he could not deny was very much like the old style.

I have only recently discovered in Part XXXIII, Proc. S. P. R., p. 399, a discussion by Dr. Hodgson of early attempts at writing, and a footnote which reads as follows:

"Miss R. (p. 292), whose friend was apparently the first to write at all, using the hand while 'controlling' the body generally, and also using the hand while Phinuit was controlling the voice, has shown me some of this early writing and some writing of her friend when living. Some peculiarities were common to both, but not enough to found an argument upon as to the identity of the communicator."

Previous to this date, December 8, 1888, Phinuit wrote my name and his name, and Hiram Hart wrote his own name. The two styles of writing were quite dissimilar.

I have three words written by the Hart control at a still earlier date, on July 2, 1888.

All three of these instances antedate the occurrence of any writing of which I have ever seen any account. These specimens are reproduced on the facing page, with the exception that I have given only one of the three words mentioned as coming on the very earliest date.

It will be noticed that on Dec. 8, 1888, a new way of spelling the Christian name "Hiram" occurs. There was more or less joking about this afterwards between myself and the control Hart, the latter insisting upon it that he really did know how to spell his own Christian name. I am sure that such inaccuracies as this, especially in early attempts at automatic writing, can now be easily explained by the experienced investigator who is himself a psychologist; or, rather, I should say that if they cannot be explained — since I believe the trance itself is not yet really explained — they form no hindrance to the acceptance of the theory, in a general way, that

WRITTEN BY HIRAM HART, July 2, 1888

WRITTEN BY HIRAM HART, May 23, 1891

WRITTEN BY DR. PHINUIT May 23, 1891

WRITTEN BY MRS. PIPER, May 23, 1891
In her normal state after coming out of trance

WRITTEN BY DR. PHINUIT, Dec. 8, 1888

WRITTEN BY DR. PHINUIT, Dec. 8, 1888

WRITTEN BY HIRAM HART, Dec. 8 1888

intelligences on the Other Side are endeavoring to communicate with intelligences on this side, through an intermediary, by the ordinary method of handwriting.

In the winter of 1892–3 came the extremely interesting series of sittings arranged by Dr. Hodgson for the express purpose of obtaining further communications from that remarkable personality, George Pelham, who died in the preceding February, and made himself known to some of his friends within a few weeks after his death. The history of the early G. P. communications, as they are called, is given in detail by Dr. Hodgson in Part XXXIII of the S. P. R. Proceedings, February, 1898, with which all students of psychical research are doubtless familiar. The sittings of this series took place in the evening, when I was able to attend as reporter. It is needless to say that all this work was most interesting and fascinating to me, and I considered myself specially favored in having opportunity to perform it.

In September, 1895, I had my last conversation with the personality known as Dr. Phinuit, though of course I did not know at the time that it was to be my last, or I should have felt that I was taking leave of a dear faithful friend. There was an interval of four years during which I had no sittings. Mrs. Piper was ill a portion of the time and was not giving sittings, and when she did give them I was not knowing to all that was going on in the affairs of the trance. I knew that it had taken on an entirely new phase, that the number of sitters had been reduced to a comparatively small one. I learned later that strange things *had* taken place, and that in the course of the year 1897 Dr. Phinuit was displaced by other controls, and a new régime was established. I presumed there was so much of greater importance of which Dr. Hodgson had charge, in the conduct of his work, that my small affairs had been lost sight of altogether. I feared I had had my last talk with my old friend Hiram Hart. In fact, I thought my connection with the Piper work had come to an end, whereas the truth is that by far the most important part of it was to come.

It was in the fall of 1899 that I resigned my position in the police department, and for a period of about three months I enjoyed a rest from routine work. Hardly had I found myself at leisure when Dr. Hodgson asked for my assistance to make copy of a volume of records of communications which had been received in the course of the two preceding seasons and after the important change in the mediumship had taken place. Much of this matter proved to be most fascinating reading and the volume had for me an absorbing interest. For a few brief weeks just at this time I was living absolutely alone in a good-sized apartment, the friend with whom I shared the apartment being absent temporarily. If a diary kept during these weeks had recorded that I "rose betimes, breakfasted, copied, lunched, copied, supped, copied, retired," it would not have been far from the truth. And I went to my bed singing and slept the sleep of a child. While one world was entirely, in accordance with my wish, shut out by the brick walls of my own apartment, I myself was being introduced to a new and different world. There were in these records descriptions of life on the Other Side of the Veil, supposed to be given by one or more persons whose names are well known to English speaking people, which were most entertaining. But of these matters I am not privileged nor do I wish to speak in detail here. They are private records now in the possession of the English S. P. R., the publication of which lies in the discretion of the Council of that body. Suffice it to say that I could not lay the volume down for more than a moment at a time, but kept it in my hand from morning till night.

While this work was going on or when nearly finished I was surprised one day to receive a note from Dr. Hodgson saying that I might have a sitting. I went to the Heights on Dec. 20, 1899, Dr. Hodgson accompanying me. I was practically introduced on that day to the group of personalities on the Other Side who have been, as it appears, managing the communications from that side ever since, among whom "Imperator" is supposed to be the leader, "Rector" the amanuensis and interpreter, who controls and looks after the organism generally while the psychic is entranced, "Prudens," "Grocyn," and the "Doctor" members, all evidently assumed appellations; to which group George Pelham, F. W. H. Myers, and one or two others whose names are prominent have from time to time been added; to say nothing of numerous lesser lights, friends and relatives of individual sitters whom they have been and still are trying to reach.

The reader who is not familiar with these matters is referred to past regular publications of the English S. P. R., also to a book called "Spirit Teachings," published by William Stainton Moses under the pseudonym of M. A. Oxon, London, 1883; a remarkable book which is full of the spiritual teachings of the trance personality calling itself Imperator.

At this first sitting under the new régime, behold my old friend Hiram Hart appeared once more. Dr. Hodgson left the room temporarily while I conversed with my friend. He had neither progressed out of remembrance of me, it seems, nor had he been unfaithful to early ties, but the moment there was opportunity he was on hand. He asked if I knew that he had been calling for me for a long time, but in reply to my question said he had been told why I could not come. The method of communication on this occasion was by writing. My friend made some of his peculiar H's, and when I said, "Hodgson doesn't believe in those H's, does he?" he replied: "I do not know or care; I know I am I . . . . and that is I am Hiram Hart."

There were statements made to me at this and a second sitting occurring a few weeks later which proved in the light of subsequent events to be so important that they mark an epoch in my life. But these I shall have to reserve for a further chapter.

VI

ASSOCIATION WITH A. P. MARTIN

1894

In 1894 Augustus P. Martin was appointed to the chairmanship of the board of police and came to the office where I had already served nine years. I had never previously met him, though from his having been for a long time prominent in the commercial and social life of Boston I knew him by reputation and had seen him in his accustomed place on Sundays at church. At one time he had been mayor of the city. In fact, it was just ten years previous to this that he had served as mayor, and it was during the year immediately following his term of office that the amendments to the city charter, previously mentioned, went into force, under which the board of police was created, to which he now came as its head.

The five years of his term of office as head of the police department were crowded full of serious and responsible work for him, and I was allowed to have my share in it as one of his assistants. During those five years I seemed to be living under a sort of paternalism, different from anything I had ever

AUGUSTUS P. MARTIN

IN HIS FIFTIETH YEAR

known. He was in public office what I imagine an old Roman patrician might have been. He was like a father to all young people who were in the employ of the department of which he had charge, especially to women. The invasion of the business world by women had taken place mostly in his day and he believed that this step was freighted with incalculable benefit to both sexes.

He had the faculty of appealing to and calling out the best in his subordinates. The geniality of his nature and the kindly courtesy of his manner made themselves felt like sunlight in the quarters which he occupied daily, and during all my experience in office life I have never known a man more loved by other men than was he. Men were glad to come, if for a few brief moments only, into the warmth of his presence, and seldom one left it without feeling better for it. This is not my own prejudiced opinion merely, for I have heard his occupancy of a public chair characterized as "dignity, sweetness and light."

He listened patiently to the complaint of the poorest petitioner for justice or applicant for assistance, and in cases which called for the rendering of a judgment he generally showed himself possessed of a wisdom and a sense of justice such that his friends often jokingly told him that he had missed his calling in life and should have been a judge on the bench.

But with all his gentleness of manner and kindness of heart, his mentality was original and forceful. He did not always follow in the footsteps of his predecessors. It was his habit first to decide upon what policy it was best to pursue, and then, if ordinary methods were not adequate for putting the policy into effect, to devise others. Not that he never erred in judgment or in conduct. In fact, he was one of the most natural human beings I have ever known, and humanity does err. His naturalness was his charm. But, I am not writing a biography.

The General — for as such he was popularly known — left the police department at the expiration of his term of office, in the spring of 1899, and it was in the fall of that same year that I gave up my position also. The association seemed to have come to an end. Oct. 5 was the date of my leaving. On Oct. 16 a certain psychic [Mrs. G.] whom I saw occasionally told me that I was to go back to my old position, that something more was to be required of me, and on Nov. 30 another psychic [Mrs. S.] told me practically the same thing. They were both very positive in their statements, and both said I was to go back for a short time only. I set these predictions down at once as incorrect, for my feeling against returning was so strong that I thought no possible inducement could take me back. On Dec. 13 I had persuaded General Martin, who was then at leisure at his home, to accompany me on a visit to one of these same psychics [Mrs. S.], who prophesied for him, in plain language, that another high office or position was to be offered him. Then came my first private sitting with Mrs. Piper under the new régime, previously mentioned, which took place on Dec. 20, at which I was accompanied by Dr. Hodgson.

Dr. Hodgson had chided me, taking the ground of worldly wisdom, for having resigned the position I had held so long, not understanding all my reasons for so doing, but when I appealed to Imperator as to whether I had done right or wrong, the latter unhesitatingly replied:

" Right, and made the way for a new life, new scenes, new enterprises, new conditions, whereby thou wilt be completely thine own master. Regret not thy act."

And Dr. Hodgson had, of course, to submit to the opinion of the personality for whom he had so great a respect. In speaking of future work Imperator said:

" There are many that are thy friends and who would give thee much help and will without any effort of thine own, remember, friend. We often say seek and ye shall find. In this case we say seek not, and if we be obeyed, every detail will be made known to thee. We [see thee] receiving communications from thy past surroundings which will verify all we now give utterance to."

It happened that Josiah Quincy, who was mayor of Boston that year, just before leaving the mayor's chair and as almost his last official act, appointed General Martin to the position of water commissioner for the city, which position he accepted and took up his duties in the beginning of the year 1900. This was a complete surprise to me, and I understand was an equal surprise to the appointee. On Jan. 12 I received a request from the new water commissioner to present myself at City Hall for the purpose of rendering him some assistance, although not then as an employee of the department. On the very same day, the 12th, to my astonishment I received a letter from Dr. Hodgson saying that Imperator had especially asked him to arrange another sitting for me with Mrs. Piper, that I was to go alone, that it was important for my own good, after which it might not be necessary for me to go again for some time.

I went to City Hall on the 15th. I did not feel at all certain in my own mind that it was best to engage myself in a position there permanently. Imperator had hinted new fields, new scenes, etc. I was a little puffed up by these suggestions, and, although it was a pleasure to assist General Martin in any kind of work, I secretly hoped that my service in government departments had come to an end, that the monotony of my life was to be broken, and that I might take wing for some distant spot, I cared not where.

On the 17th I went again to Mrs. Piper. Imperator said:

" Thou art being cared for in all ways and we have thy interests at stake, friend, and we are leading thee in the right way now. Let us tell thee that within a few short weeks thou wilt see a great change in thy life for the *very* best. A position will be given thee without thy seeking it. As we were closing our last meeting we saw a light before thee of which we could not then speak and we have chosen this opportunity to do so."

Very shortly after this I was appointed to a position in the water department and the old association was renewed, City Hall being only a stone's throw from the old locality. I therefore considered that the prophecy made by the two psychics was almost literally fulfilled. Imperator, however, seemed to see this still more clearly, and said: " We warn thee not to re-enter the former surroundings, we desire thee to keep apart from it altogether, and we ask thee to dare not disobey our leadings." He had seen me "receiving communications from my past surroundings," which was correct, but did not see me going back to the identical position in the police department. All three psychics saw the same event, which was to take place and did take place, Mrs. Piper seeing it more clearly than the other two psychics, as I reread my notes to-day.

I have thought best to give these items in detail in this particular instance, since they all are so closely related. The subject of foresight, however, is one on which I do not wish to express here any definite opinion whatever, nor to assume an understanding of it. Coming events cast their shadows before, which we ourselves, with our normal sight, can sometimes perceive. It is human, especially when one is in trouble or doubt, to want to know something about what is to take place, but it is not dignified to seek to know about the future to the extent of having one's serenity disturbed in the performance of the duty of the day. In fact, it seems to me that it is only in the conscientious performance of the daily duty, without undue anxiety about the future, that desirable changes are brought about. We bring them about ourselves. We work steadily toward them and by some occult law we draw to ourselves that which we really need, that of which we are deserving and for which we are prepared. Outward affairs, in the life of a serious-minded person, seem to follow and correspond with inward change and growth.

VII

APPARENT FAILURE OF PREDICTION

1900–1902

To go back to the sitting of Jan. 17, 1900, with Mrs. Piper, mentioned in the preceding chapter. Of all the sittings which I can remember, this one made the deepest impression upon me. After a few lines of script the pencil was dropped from the psychic's hand and the voice taken, and for nearly two hours conversation was carried on. Before the time was up I threw away my own pen and paper, gave up the effort to take notes, and had a heart to heart talk with the trance personalities.

It was my first experience with Rector's use of the voice. His style differed so greatly from the familiar style of Phinuit, or even from that of my friend Hiram Hart, that I realized at once that I was conversing with a different individuality. He was so dignified, so kind, so sympathetic, so serious, so desirous of assisting me to lift my life to a higher level, that I was almost overcome. How these newly found spirits, whoever they might be, should know so much about me, I could not understand. I thought myself a stranger to them, but they seemed to know me through and through. They saw in me capacity which I only half recognized in myself, and they seemed to think me worthy of their time, their effort, their assistance, and they endeavored to convince me of the fact that my life was of some importance and must not be undervalued by me. The period of fourteen years in one spot, just then ended, had seemed long and difficult to me, yet Imperator now called it " only a short school for thee." So brief evidently do the decades seem to the discarnate eye which takes in the wider span.

Hiram Hart came and said: " Oh, I bless the day when I found you here. I do not see you very often now. I come here and take a look and do not see you and then go away." " Here " means at the scene of operations, the point of communication, which is always where Mrs. Piper happens for the time to be located.

But the most important statement made to me by Imperator on this occasion, in speaking of my again being associated with General Martin, was the following:

" We see thee and him writing a book *together*."

I asked: " What about? "

" It is concerning the natural things in life and many different conditions of thy life, which will be put together in a form of philosophy. *It will be so* in spite of anything which thou mayst think to the contrary."

It was true we were able to work well together, or so at least I flattered myself. Both the commercial world and the official world to-day are full of just such combinations of men as directors and women as right-hand assistants. A woman serving in the capacity of private secretary to a man whose mind is filled with the affairs of his office and whose time is precious should be able to adapt herself to his peculiarities, complement his weaknesses, and stand respectfully and safely aside from his strength. Women have an intuitive perception of these things, and even a young woman who has not had experience is often easily able to adjust herself to the requirements of such a position. At any rate, when in a haphazard selection the right combination is formed, a better than the ordinary grade of work ought to be expected and more than the usual amount can be accomplished.

I will say here that as far back as when I was at school I made up my mind that, whatever else I did, I would not attempt to become an author. That was not to be my field. Others were more naturally fitted for it. I must have other work to do. Later in life, when I found myself struggling along in doubt and mental darkness, and occasionally the solution of some problem would relieve my mind,

I flattered myself secretly that sometime I might gather together into a sort of whole the solutions of the various problems which had presented themselves to me, and inflict the mass in printed form upon others. Still later, I came to the conclusion that every problem, without exception, with which I had battled had been met and solved ages before I was born; I found that the wisdom of all the great philosophers had been handed down and was accessible to all who could read, and therefore I again dropped the idea of ever entering the field of authorship. Not that it is a difficult thing in these days to write and publish a book of some kind, but I concluded that there were *too many* books in the world. The world be better off if there were only half as many. But when Imperator marked out my path for me in the manner above given, I confess to at least a little surprise, and on another later occasion, when I remarked to him that I did not wish to publish a book simply from a sense of duty, he replied:

"Friend, to write a book, it is thy doom or duty, one and both combined."

I did not speak of this particular matter to General Martin. He was eager to hear all I was willing to report, but while I gave him much, I also withheld much. I simply told him in a general way that it was said we were yet to do some special work together. I was afraid and ashamed to tell him. I had long before learned to keep prophecies to myself until I saw some sign of their fulfilment. He was a man of family ties, of many cares, burdens and responsibilities both in his private and public life, and especially when illness came upon him I could see no possible way by which any work of that kind could be done.

I will say here that he did not specially pursue the subject of Spiritism in the sense of seeking mediums and paying attention to what they had to say, yet he was altogether too open-minded and simple-hearted to scoff at it. Soon after my making his acquaintance he related to me an interesting experience of his own which happened very soon after the death of his mother, who died when he was a young man of about twenty-one, and to whom he had been attached with more than the usual devotion of son to mother. A servant in the family, young and quite ignorant, gave indications of being controlled by the spirit of his mother within a short time after her passing out, giving her maiden name — Verrall — a very uncommon name, and one which the servant could not possibly have known. I cannot relate the incident in full, my point being that it made an ineradicable impression upon his mind and was sufficiently serious to cause him to refrain from speaking lightly of such matters when he found any one deeply interested in them, had he otherwise been inclined to do so.

During middle life he attended the church of the Rev. Minot J. Savage for something over twenty years, rarely missed a Sunday and took a leading part in the management of church affairs. He was an admirer of Mr. Savage's independent thinking, and all the old attendants at that church know that there was a great deal of what might be called Spiritualism in Mr. Savage's sermons.

He sat in his chair at City Hall for somewhat over a year, then one day in March, 1901, he was taken ill and obliged to remain at his home. He was, however, continued in office by two mayors, Thomas N. Hart and Patrick A. Collins. This was one way in which his conspicuous service of the past, to both city and country, was recognized by some of his friends, citizens of Boston of substantial character, who had power and influence in the management of public affairs. But I wish to state here, in justice to him, that during almost the entire length of his illness his mind remained clear, he was knowing to all the important affairs of the department of which he had charge, and himself dictated its policy. It devolved upon me to travel back and forth frequently, almost daily, between City Hall and his residence in the suburbs, carrying bills and papers of all kinds, getting his signature to them and taking back his orders. I remember one instance in particular when he dictated an important letter, assigning newly appointed subordinates to their respective places and duties, a letter which was remarked upon when I took it back to the office for the clearness and terseness of its expression and for the authority which it conveyed.

But this was a weary summer, that of 1901. The suffering sick were languishing in the extreme heat, and for the well there was the dead monotony of life's drudgery and the heart-sickness which comes from hope deferred. I had not had access to Mrs. Piper since November of the preceding year. The trance personalities had not sent for me, and it was not my habit at that time to ask for sittings. All signs seemed to be failing, and the ground which I had thought solid seemed to be slipping again from beneath my feet. I think, however, Dr. Hodgson made it known that I desired a sitting, and on Jan. 13, 1902, at a sitting of his own, the following came:

"Also Miss Robbins' friends hath tried in vain to reach her. I, Rector, in particular. But, friend, we fail to reach through lights [1] sufficiently to give our messages clearly."

Dr. Hodgson replied: "She thought she got a few words I believe from you through another light."

[1] "Light" is the word commonly used by the trance personalities for "psychic" or "medium."

Rector said: "Imperator sent me several times but I was not sure that I had reached her."

This certainly implies that Imperator and his group do try or have tried on occasions to communicate through other "lights" when there is special need of their reaching those over whom they assume to have charge. What they do in the way of experiment is another matter. I had recognized on one or two occasions what appeared to be an attempt on the part of Rector to communicate with me through natural but undeveloped psychics. I *felt strongly* that such an attempt was being made.

A sitting was arranged for me, to take place about a week later, on Jan. 22. From that time on, for the next two months, I was constantly receiving through Dr. Hodgson messages from Imperator and Rector and sending messages to them. For, strange as it may seem, although the sick man whom all these messages concerned knew very little, almost nothing, about Imperator and his group, the latter apparently took a very great interest in him. I delivered to him a few messages which I thought might give him hope and comfort, and I think I must certainly have given him the impression that my own feeling, in spite of all misunderstandings, was that just as soon as he passed through and emerged from the shadow of death there would be for him a welcome on the Other Side of which he little dreamed. At least, that was my hope.

But the important point here in its relation to psychical research is that I believed, from the many emphatic statements made to me by a group of spirits, that I was to be required in the future to assist in a field of work which *they* considered most important, that there was a particular person with whom I was to be associated in that work perhaps more closely than with any other, yet that particular person was dying.

While the object I have in view compels me to speak freely of serious things, I trust no one will dream that there is aught in my heart but the utmost reverence for everything associated with that most mysterious change through which all human beings must pass and which comes to none but once. Although I had been bereft of certain relatives and friends, it had not hitherto fallen to my lot to sit often or long at the bedside of the sick. But to watch a fellow-creature who is gradually and surely approaching the end of life, who will not stay his feet for protest, tear or prayer, to almost see the soul as it plumes its wings for flight, is certainly an experience which should produce the greatest awe in the heart and the mind of the watcher.

The actual date of the passing out was March 13, 1902.

While General Martin was a man widely known in his own city, he had little reputation which extended beyond this limit, except in connection with the War of the Rebellion, in which he served during its entire continuance. He was complimented by General Meade for distinguished service at the Battle of Gettysburg. It was on the third and last day of this memorable and terrific fight that his battery, which had been located with immense difficulty on the summit of a rugged hill, had a clear sweep of the open field over which Pickett's Division of the Confederate Army made its famous charge, rank after rank of which were mowed down by the steady firing from Little Round Top, and the tide of battle was turned.

The Boston Transcript said of him at the time of his death: "Hardly any other of Boston's citizens was better known, and few had contributed more than he of time, talent and activity to the military and civic service and functions of the city. . . . He fitted best into those free movements of citizens called into being by special occasions, and expressive of local patriotism and public spirit. It was the recognition of this fitness that secured his selection as chief marshall upon two of the most prominent commemorative occasions within the last quarter-century, and he was sure to be prominent in all projects for the development and improvement of his city."

He was not a general in the army, nor did that title rightfully belong to him until the year 1882, when Governor John D. Long, afterwards Secretary of the United States Navy, upon whose staff he was serving at the time, commissioned him, lawfully, Brigadier General, in recognition of his valuable services during the war. Another newspaper article which appeared at the time of his death says: "Tardy justice was thus done and he thereafter bore a title truthfully which he had long borne by courtesy."

It may be evident later that the title which best fits a person's character, the name by which he has been most intimately known and by which he is most endeared, clings to him after he has passed to the Other Side.

VIII

FULFILMENT

1903–1907

March 13, 1902, must be borne in mind as an important date in this narration. It marked the passing of a life from this earth. A few days after the occurrence I saw Dr. Hodgson and instructed him particularly not to mention my name in any way at the Piper trance, as it is sometimes called. I felt that, as matters stood between myself and the trance personalities, there had been to say the least some misunderstanding and confusion, and that the only dignified course for me to pursue was to ask no favors and abide my time. I thought this my opportunity, too, to test the value once more of what had seemed to be a close relation between myself and personalities whom I knew only as a part of the Unseen.

No word or hint came for me during the remainder of that season, and almost another whole season passed when one day, May 21, 1903, at a sitting of Dr. Hodgson's, in one of those significant mutterings of Mrs. Piper's when coming out of trance, when she seems to be returning to her body, taking last glimpses of people in the spirit whom she designates as "white people," while those to whom she is returning appear to her "black," she said:

"General Martin says he is coming here pretty soon to speak — Martin — love to — this is a pretty dark place after all."

Nothing more until Dec. 15 of that same year, when the following conversation took place between Rector and Dr. Hodgson while arrangements were being made for future sittings, Rector's words being quoted from the automatic script, Dr. Hodgson's being enclosed in the round brackets: —

"There is a spirit here who calls constantly for a lady in the body whom he refers to as —"

[Hand enquires of Spirit?]

"R o b b i n s."

(Yes. She will doubtless be rejoiced to come. She said long ago that she was waiting for anything that came.)

"This is Imperator's arrangement for the spirit who spake unto Him to give him relief."

(Yes.)

"Imperator hath referred to it several times and called our attention to it but He hath not really commanded us until now, as He hath been assisting the spirit."

"Wilt thou attend to this friend on the earthly side and appoint for a meeting with us on the third after coming?"

(Yes, I will.)

[" Third after coming " means the third day after the coming Sabbath.]

A sitting was then arranged for me, to take place on Dec. 23d, about twenty-one months after the passing out. Behold, my old friend, business associate and employer appears, communicates as clearly and strongly as if he had had many previous opportunities instead of having had none, and at this very first opportunity says:

" I want to know if you don't think we could manage to write a book? "

And later, on the same occasion:

" I have had this on my mind ever since I came into this world and I would like to have it carried out."

Still later:

" It has got to be. It is a thing that I am bound to have."

I ask:

(You mean that you are bound I shall publish a book?)

The reply came:

" Literally, absolutely, out and out, with pen, paper and ink, write a book and publish it, and I am going to be the inspirer and instigator of it, and we are going to write that book together just as sure as you live."

What! Was it then true that the line of work marked out four years previously was after all to be pursued, no hindrance having occurred in the meantime except — except — *except* — DEATH!!

My sittings with Mrs. Piper continued from that time on, taking place, however, rarely. I was directed from the beginning to withhold some of my communications from Dr. Hodgson, although I gave him the greater part of them. He could not himself always understand the full purpose of my relation to the trance personalities, or why a certain day should be assigned to me rather than to some one else who could give more substantial aid to the investigations that were being carried on in the name of science, or some one who, perhaps, received better communications and more matter that was evidential in its nature than my own. But it is well known that he came in time to obey implicitly the wishes of the trance personalities in making arrangements for the different sitters, and I am told that he was heard to remark in his emphatic way, in regard to an appointment for me: *"If they wish it, so it shall be."*

I do not claim any "inspiration" in anything I say or do. Nor do I disclaim it. I simply do not know. In the first place, I would not be guilty of putting upon any spirit, either friend or stranger, the responsibility for something *no better* than what I can do. In the second place, if I do anything that is worthy, especially after long preparation and with much effort, I am human enough still to want a little credit for it, for myself. I fondly dreamed that I might become one of those scribes who have only to hold the pencil for language to flow with fluency from the tips of their fingers. But not so. I might sit for an hour at a time in silent expectation, and not until there was a conscious effort on my part to move the pencil would it show the slightest inclination to stir.

However, to say that I am *not* conscious of the coöperation of friends in the Unseen in any part of my work would not be strictly true. I am often conscious of their presence. Apart from the recognition within one's own spirit, there are at times delicate changes in or subtle states of the nervous system which come gradually to be recognized by the highly sensitive organization as sure indices of the closeness of other beings, though we cannot point the finger at them or clasp them by the hand. I feel sure from conversations I have had with others that this fact lies within the experience of many people who will recognize the truth of what I say, impossible as it is to define such experience with sufficient precision to make it understood by one who has never known it.

On December 1, 1905, the many friends of Dr. Richard Hodgson were astounded at seeing in the morning papers the announcement of his sudden death, which occurred the preceding evening. It is safe to say that there was not a man in the city of Boston who took better care of his health, who derived more pleasure from athletic sports, who felt more pride in keeping his physique up to its highest standard. He purified his body and his life for his special work, and I feel that I am within bounds of the strictest veracity when I say that in and through that work higher ideals of living were continually being presented to his mind. He was not ashamed to say that he followed the advice of an "Imperator" or of some other unseen intelligence even in matters pertaining to physical well-being, although I think no one who ever saw him could say that he had aught but the greatest respect for his own good judgment which was plainly indicated upon his brow.

The day of his death happened to be my opportunity at Arlington Heights. I had a sitting in the morning and he died in the very early evening of the same day. No hint of what was to take place reached me from the Other Side. Mrs. Piper, who had just entered upon her work for the season, was much shocked by the occurrence. I spent an hour at her bedside on the evening of the day after the death, and she related to me a most interesting dream which she had the preceding night. It was, in brief, as follows:

She seemed to be approaching a large dark tunnel. At its entrance, appearing from the inside, stood a man who waved his hand at her with a motion which seemed to say: "Keep back, do no enter this tunnel." She related her dream early the next morning to members of her family, remarking as she did so that the *hand* looked like Dr. Hodgson's hand and its peculiar motion was like his. It was not until after she had told her dream that the morning paper containing the news of the death was laid upon her bed. Of course I was ready at once with my own interpretation of the dream, which seemed to me a most significant one, namely, that Dr. Hodgson's first thought, on finding that he had himself traversed the dark passage leading from this world to the other, was to turn back to impress upon her the importance of the fact that her time had not yet come, that her work was not yet finished.

I took down the dream at her dictation and afterwards secured its corroboration by her daughters. I handed this record in to the authorities, but have never seen or heard of any reference to the dream since that time. My own interpretation of it, however, certainly harmonizes with a message which purported to come for Mrs. Piper from Dr. Hodgson himself later in that winter at one of my own sittings; for, strange as it may seem, though many messages come through her, seldom one comes for her. He said:

"Will you give my love to Mrs. Piper and tell her that I wish her to *cling to the rigging,* and tell her to go on unceasingly, untiringly, and everything will win out."

I attended Dr. Hodgson's funeral on Dec. 23, 1905. On Jan. 1, 1906, eight days later, when passing out of my house in the morning and glancing at the accustomed place for my mail, what was my astonishment at seeing an envelope addressed to myself in the familiar and peculiar handwriting of Dr. Hodgson. It startled even me a little, to whom life and death have become the same. The envelope contained his Christmas card. He had for some years been in the habit of sending to his friends, at Christmas, cards with a few lines or a stanza of poetry printed thereon, an accompaniment to his good wishes for the season. I learned later that the envelopes were found all addressed, ready for the Christmas mail, and about ten days after his death his executors had them mailed. This particular selection, lines from Tennyson, was so appropriate to the occasion and the circumstances that I will insert it here:

> Let be thy wail, and help thy fellow-men,
> And make thy gold thy vassal, not thy king,
> And fling free alms into the beggar's bowl,
> And send the day into the darken'd heart;

Nor list for guerdon in the voice of men,
A dying echo from a falling wall;
* * * * * * *

And lay thine uphill shoulder to the wheel,
And climb the Mount of Blessing, whence, if
thou
Look higher, then — perchance — thou mayest
— beyond
A hundred ever-rising mountain lines,
And past the range of Night and Shadow — see
The high-heaven dawn of more than mortal day
Strike on the Mount of Vision!

Surely a call to duty if ever there were one, a clarion call from the Mount of Vision itself, which he had already climbed.

Dr. Hodgson occupied an unique position in Boston in relation to other people who were interested in psychical research, and especially to those who had access to Mrs. Piper. He was the centre of a group. He was the centre of a circle. Each member of the circle placed in him the utmost confidence, a trust he was never known to betray Yet, while his acquaintance extended to all, there was not a general acquaintance among the members of the group. They formed a sort of chain to which his relation was the connecting link. But when he fell, a half-dozen or more sitters immediately joined hands to see to it that the chain should not entirely fall apart; to see that all papers and reports confidentially placed in his keeping should be properly safeguarded; and, perhaps more important than all else, to see that the "Light," so called, should be carefully watched and that opportunities for further experiment should if possible be offered, now that he was on the Other Side instead of on this.

I discovered then that there were at least a few people who, while recognizing fully the scientific importance of this work, had at the same time received from the Other Side of the Veil a spiritual uplifting which meant almost their salvation.

To return to my sitting of Dec. 20 of this same year (1905), a date which marks an epoch in the annals of psychical research in this country. While conversing with my communicator I remarked that I would like to tell the gentleman at the head of the state department in which I was employed something about my private work. I thought it was due him to be told something about the nature of the outside matters which occasionally took me away from my post, that it was no more than courtesy on my part to inform him. Moreover, I took him to be a man who would not allow himself to be prejudiced against the subject, whether familiar with it or not, and who might even take an interest it it. The reply was:

"It would be a little unwise at the present time, . . . it might weaken his respect for you along the intellectual lines, . . . but there is a time for everything, and the truth will bear its weight and it will work its way through all the dark clouds and win its way into the light, and leave this to time, and the time will present itself when you can speak openly on the question and not be considered inferior intellectually, and that is what I do not wish. I am determined that you shall be respected."

These remarks, unimportant though they may seem, turned out very shortly to be truly prophetic in their nature. Dr. Hodgson died on the evening of that very day. I did not know of the death until some time the following day. At the very first sitting which took place after the death, given to a gentleman who had been a close friend of Dr. Hodgson's and familiar with his work for years, the trance personalities mentioned the names of various persons who, in the emergency which had arisen, could be of service in what they call "*their* work," and my name was one of the number. My assistance, however, was not actually requested by those in charge on *this* side until about two months later.

It must be remembered by the uninitiated that the more highly developed the psychic and the deeper the trance into which she passes, the more delicate, apparently, are the conditions pertaining to that state, and the greater the watchfulness required on the part of the sitter. And in this particular case the spirit controls are somewhat autocratic. They will have this and they will not have that. They will allow this person and they will not allow that person. It is wholly against their wishes, for reasons probably still best known to themselves, that strangers should be introduced without their express consent. And sometimes they say in as many words that if their wishes in certain matters are not complied with they will "refuse to come," which evidently means that Mrs. Piper would not be able to go into the trance state at her pleasure and there would be no sitting. The control of affairs is practically from the Other Side, however much we may like to ignore the fact.

About this time, two months after the death, some one in authority on this side, on his own initiative, consulted with the governor of the commonwealth and the chief of the department where I was engaged — by name Dr. Austin Peters — and I was briefly informed that I might absent myself on occasional days for the special purpose of assisting in the Piper work, *provided* that my absence was "not detrimental to the public service," and provided, also, that time thus taken should be charged against the vacation days of the year which were due me. I found that Dr. Peters, while unfamiliar with psychial research as such, recognized the importance of any work done in the name of science. During the remainder of the season, therefore, I was present at many of the sittings and assisted in keeping the records.

The subject having been brought to my attention in the manner explained, instead of my being obliged to bring it to the attention of others, and my pathway thus made easy, was all the fulfilment that I desired of the prophetic words uttered through the trance two months previously.

It appears, then, that respect for psychical research still depends somewhat — at least in an opinion expressed from the Other Side — upon whether the work be initiated and backed by some one high in social standing or official life, or whether it be pursued by some one lower down in the scale of position. But let us be thankful that search in this interesting and important field *has* at last become respectable, no matter by whom it has been made so.

During the winter of 1906-7 Mrs. Piper was in England giving sittings under the auspices of the English S. P. R. at its rooms in London. [See Proc. Part LVII, Vol. XXII, October, 1908.] The winter of 1907-8 she spent in Boston. I was called early in the season for a sitting. My communicator appears, tells me that "delays are dangerous," and that he wishes me to lose no time in the gathering together of my scattered papers in preparation for publication.

IX

FAITH

I do not like the word "belief" as it is commonly used, and I have tried to extirpate it from my vocabulary; not, however, with perfect success. When a person puts the direct question to me, "Do you believe such and such a thing," and expects me to answer yes or no, I feel that by answering "yes" I am committing myself to a state of mind so positive that it shuts out further light on the point in question. Many times I have answered: "I neither believe nor disbelieve; I *think* it is so, but do not know." For that is what the word means, an acceptance of an opinion or a fact without personal knowledge of its truth. The word is associated in my mind with an ignorant assent, and after throwing away dogmatic belief in early years I have tried to keep my mind open for whatever of new there might come into it, and not make hasty judgments. I want to *know* things. Some things I do know and can prove their truth to others. Many other things are for me practically true, though I can *not* prove their truth to others. They *appear* to me to be true, and the appearance is so strong that it practically amounts to a belief, so that I can hardly dispense with the word after all. But to believe a thing without any knowledge at all, either the knowledge that comes from a clear inner light or an outward experience, is something that is contrary to my nature, and when I am expected to answer yes or no to a direct question about belief, I want to have some idea of what the person who puts the question means by the word.

The expression " inner light " has no meaning for many people, but for some it has a very great significance. Inner light sometimes makes a truth so clear, to the person possessing the light, that it is impossible for him not to believe it even before outward experience has confirmed it, and though all the world may for the moment say " you are wrong."

During the larger portion of the first busy decade of which I have spoken, after swinging onto a ground of no definite religious belief of any kind, I, too, was privileged to sit under the liberalizing, optimistic and truly spiritual teaching of the Rev. Minot J. Savage, then occupying a pulpit in Boston. The seeming deadness to me of everything outside of the senses was gradually lessening, and a new kind of faith in a future life was budding; not one which had been handed down to me from my ancestors, but one which was destined in time to become more real, and my experiences in Spiritism, so called, probably helped on considerably the growth of this new faith. I would not give the impression that from the very beginning I actually believed in all that purported to come from the spirit world, but with long continued experience, and a fidelity on the part of friends on the Other Side which seems *never to fail,* conviction grows, it fastens itself upon one and cannot be shaken off.

Belief in a future life is, as William James puts it, " largely a matter of personal feeling." It is, I think, a matter of individual apprehension and appropriation, based partly upon experience in what purports to be communion of some sort with the so-called dead, and partly upon an indefinable quality of the soul which is able to appropriate from the Vastness outside of itself, a quality variable in its potency in different individuals and which one person cannot impart to another. I might offer page after page of communications, yet they would never mean to one who sees them only in the cold type what they mean to me. Personal experience of this kind, therefore, may be a very large factor in the gradual growth of belief, yet not the only factor and perhaps not the most important. The layman who is eager and thirsting for the truth cannot wait for the dictum of Science, and if to him truth is revealed in some surer and quicker way than by the slow process of scientific experimentation, no one may easily rob him of the personal satisfaction which he derives from such revelation.

As one after another of my friends have gone to the spirit world they have in turn become such a vital part of my every-day consciousness that I think about them and speak of them as if they were still actually in my circle of acquaintance and only temporarily out of my sight. I believe that I do converse with them, perhaps not in the "fullness of their personality," or the "same fullness of clear consciousness that they exhibited during life," but that I do converse with them; that there is, not always, but on many occasions, a clear and distinct understanding between me and my communicator, and a sense of gratification on my part as of having met and exchanged greetings with some dear old friend. I do not think, however, that if I had not had opportunity with some of the most gifted and highly developed psychics I should ever have become possessed of so strong a sense of reality and gratification. This I say with the greatest respect for those who possess the psychic gift in a lesser degree.

It was not until the passing of the friend who went last to the spirit world that I seemed somehow to come into the blessedness of thinking mostly about life and excluding death altogether from my thoughts, of feeling life in the air which I breathe, the sky which I look at, the sun which shines upon me, and the darkness which shrouds and rests me; in fact, life and intelligence everywhere. And the wonderful thing about thus "coming into universal consciousness," as it is called, is that it takes away morbid over-anxiety to understand the whole scheme of creation or nothing, it brings back the natural charm of things which we felt in our childhood, it puts a new meaning into our common every-day life, and makes it worth while to endeavor to make of it a "thing of beauty," a "thing of power."

I do not wish to be understood as uttering any final word on the subject of prophecy, or as really offering any explanation at all. That must be left to the psychologist and the scientist. Nor do I wish any one to place any reliance whatever on predictions made by psychics from anything I may say. However important the subject of prophecy may be, the predictions themselves form a small part of the mass and the worth of the communications that come through Mrs. Piper. But I offer my personal experience, and if read aright I think it will show that the counsel given by Imperator and his group, as it affects an individual life and the spiritual significance of individual life-work, is far-seeing and wise, piercing not merely through a few years, but even through death itself.

In 1901, four years before the death of Dr.

Richard Hodgson, I communicated with him asking if he would kindly give me some information on the matter of the failure or the fulfilment of prophecy as it had come under his observation. He replied promptly and at length. At the close of the letter in which he discussed it fully for my benefit, he gave expression to his own belief in the reality of the trance personalities in language so emphatic and so beautiful that I cannot refrain from quoting it here. After his death copies of this letter were circulated among some of his most intimate friends, none of whom had seen anything quite like it written by him, and this particular passage, or rather the latter part of it, came to be known among these friends as his "confession of faith." [1]

The passage in question has not been in every instance quite accurately quoted, possibly owing to my own misinterpretation of it originally, and then to its getting into print without my having opportunity to correct it. I

[1] This has already been published, with my permission, privately at first, being included in a paper read at the annual meeting of the Tavern Club of Boston on May 6, 1906, by M. A. DeWolfe Howe, and later copied.

Those who are interested are referred to a memorial of Richard Hodgson by Dr. James H. Hyslop, Journal of the American Society for Psychical Research, Vol. I, January, 1907; and to memorials by Mrs. Henry Sidgwick and J. G. Piddington, in Proceedings of the English Society for Psychical Research, Part LII, Vol. XIX, February, 1907, in which the paper by Mr. Howe, above mentioned, is also included.

am therefore tempted to give it here in Dr. Hodgson's own peculiar chirography, which will be recognized by his many friends to whom his handwriting is familiar.

TRANSCRIPTION

November 24, 1901.

DEAR MISS ROBBINS: I should have replied to yours of 17 earlier, but could not find any copy of the notes which I now enclose in T sheets.

* * * * * * *

But apart from all this we must remember that nothing can be regarded as infallible, and I tried to put my general view about this in the notes a copy of which I enclose. About what Imperator and his group are in their world I have no doubt. They have done for me and for some others also,— more than everything, but the final written or spoken results through Mrs. P.'s inadequate organism surrounded by our earthly make-ups generally can only afford us faint glimpses of the great holies from which they take their origin. We cannot pray too much to do and suffer the will of God, whatever it be. I went through toils and turmoils and perplexities in '97 and '98 about the significance of this whole Imperator régime, but I have seemed to get on a rock after that,— I seem to understand clearly the reasons for incoherence and obscurity, etc., and I think that if for the rest of my life from now I should never see another trance or have another word from Imperator or his group,— it would make no difference to my *knowledge* that all is well, that Impera-

tor, etc., are all they claim to be and are indeed messengers that we may call divine. Be of good courage whatever happens, and pray continually, and let peace come into your soul. Why should you be distraught and worried? Everything, absolutely everything,—from a spot of ink to all the stars, every faintest thought we think up to the contemplations of the highest intelligences in the cosmos, are all in and part of the infinite Goodness. Rest in that Divine Love. All your trials are known better than you know them yourself. Do you think it is an idle word that the hairs of our heads are numbered? Have no dismay, fear nothing and trust in God.

Yours sincerely,

R. Hodgson.

I give also extracts from a second letter in reply to my acknowledgment of the above.

TRANSCRIPTION

Boston, Mass., December 1, 1901.

Dear Miss Robbins: Just a word or two in reply to your kind letter of November 27. Thanks for T document returned.

* * * * * * *

Of course we get misrepresented and misunderstood in all sorts of ways. In the old years when I was prominent in exposing fraudulent mediums, Spiritualists generally used to revile me as a gross materialistic skeptic who had no other object but the persistent determination to *disprove Spiritualism.* Nothing could have been further from the truth even then. And now, as you rightly say, in recent years, with the Imperator régime, another influence has come which I trust, even to the end and after,—with all my darkness and weakness and blunderings and brutenesses,—I shall not escape, which I trust will abide with me ever, for it is law and love and peace and freedom and joy and God.

Yours ever,

RICHARD HODGSON.

These letters speak for themselves and need no comment from me.

Let me say once more that I have been repeatedly and continually urged by those on the Other Side of the Veil, since 1900, and more especially since 1902, to offer to others something of my experience and something of the comfort which I myself have received.

And the End is Not Yet. September, 1909.

AMERICAN BRANCH

OF THE

Society for Psychical Research.

RICHARD HODGSON, LL. D.,
SECRETARY AND TREASURER,
5 BOYLSTON PLACE

FROM
RICHARD HODGSON
15 CHARLES STREET
BOSTON MASS.

Boston, Mass.. Dec 1 1901

Dear Mrs. Ritter

Just a word in time in reply to your kind letter of Nov 27. Thanks for T. book returned.

* * * * * *

Of course we get misrepresented & misunderstood in all sorts of ways. In the old years when I was prominent in exposing fraudulent mediums, Spiritualists generally used to revile me as a gross materialistic sceptic who had no other object but the unprincipled determination to disprove Spiritualism. Nothing could have been further from the truth even then. And now, as you rightly say, — in recent years, with the 'Imperator regime', another influence has come, which I trust, even to the end & after, with all my darkness & weakness & blunderings & bitternesses, — I shall not escape, which I trust will abide with me ever, — for it is Love & Love & peace & freedom & joy of God.

Yours ever

Richard Hodgson

PART II

COMMUNICATIONS FROM THE OTHER SIDE OF THE VEIL THROUGH MRS. PIPER

PART II

X

PREFATORY EXPLANATIONS

Up to the beginning of 1906 I never dreamed that I should arrive at the point of publishing reports of my own sittings with Mrs. Piper. The reports were not mine to publish, as they were all in the hands of Dr. Hodgson and he held them by right of his office as Secretary of the Society for Psychical Research. For some years previous to his death the condition on which most or all of the sittings were allowed was that a report of some kind should be made to him, every sitter, of course, retaining the right to withhold whatever was considered of too intimate and personal a character to disclose. He himself accompanied many of the sitters and made his own records. It was my habit to make very full reports. On my proposing on one occasion to omit some talk about my health, which I did not presume was of interest to any one but myself, he insisted that I should give him every word that I possibly could, saying that he had been working for years to obtain verbatim reports of these sittings, and that, of the few people whose communications came by voice, I happened to be the only one who was accustomed to the more rapid reporting. Therefore I gave him much that I would not think of allowing to be published, on the understanding between us that before he made any use of these records by way of publications of his own there would be opportunity for the reconsideration and the withholding of certain portions. I gave him these full records for the purpose of enabling him as a psychologist to form a better judgment of the value of a sitting as a whole.

He also expressed to me his opinion that in the publication of records it is better to make use of real names as far as possible rather than pseudonyms, although he recognized that there are many considerations entering into the question, and that this cannot always or perhaps often be done.

The sudden death of Dr. Hodgson altered entirely the situation of affairs. In May, 1906, the authorities, in issuing an announcement of the proposed dissolution of the American Branch of the S. P. R., made the following statement:

"The Piper records, and all documents appertaining thereto, will remain in charge of the Council of the Society; and, as promptly as the labor involved in the study of their voluminous and complicated contents will allow, a full report on the later developments of the Piper case up to the date of Dr. Hodgson's death will be issued in the *Proceedings*.

"After publication the Council of the Society will allow qualified and serious students access to the records; but only on terms which will ensure that all private and intimate matter contained in them shall be handled with proper discretion and reserve, and that all confidences shall be respected."

My own reports were included, with my consent, in the mass of documents which were transferred to London. As I am not now publishing complete records, I make this explanation to show that I have made some slight contribution to the files of the English S. P. R., and it is possible that the person who summarizes the contents of all the documents, or the "serious student" who examines them, may find in my small portion some good tests or some few points of psychological interest which I have not thought best to reproduce in this volume, my special object being to offer the running conversation rather than the test with its detailed explanation and corroboration.

The reports of my sittings are, therefore, the property of the S. P. R., and I have no right to publish without the permission of that society. On November 7, 1907, the Council of that body voted to give me permission to publish extracts from my own reports on the understanding that I should publish also an acknowledgment of the permission, together with the statement that the Council is in no way responsible for anything I may say, and I hereby absolve the Council of the Society for Psychical Research from responsibility for any and every word which I publish.

At an earlier date, September 26, 1906, I received what purported to be a communication from Richard Hodgson himself, as follows:

"If you wish to extract anything from those reports you have my consent to do so and I hope the consent of the Council."

When scientists first undertook the study of mediumistic phenomena the particular test was considered the all-important thing, and comparatively little attention was paid to anything else. More recently, voluminous and characteristic talk on the part of a communicator has been considered valuable and even evidential in its way. Professor James H. Hyslop in his work entitled "Science and a Future Life" [p. 269] says: "What we must have is psychological phenomena, and psychological phenomena of that kind which represents the systematic mental action natural to the person whose existence is in question."

Still more recently, even descriptions of life on the Other Side of the Veil, which of course cannot stand at all as positive proof of the truth of the matter, are being sought after, and I have been told by a leading psychologist that when we have a mass of non-evidential matter it will sometime have a bearing on the value of what is strictly evidential.

I am not offering my communications as "evidence" in the strict sense of that word. I am offering them simply for *what they are*, expecting that each reader of the first portion of this volume will peruse or omit this portion as he sees fit, and that each one will judge of it for himself. I realize that when I lock myself into an "upper chamber" with one other person only and that person goes into a state of unconsciousness and talks, what I bring out as a record of that talk must depend much for its value upon whatever reputation I myself may have for being a truthful recorder, if I am so fortunate as to have any.

It should be understood that in the latter years nearly all the communications coming through Mrs. Piper are in automatic writing. It is only at an occasional sitting or only for certain sitters that the communications are given through the voice. Many prefer the automatic writing, and for the purpose of scientific experimentation it is considered, I understand, more valuable. The writing that is produced can be preserved as the actual communication and cannot be disputed. However, the writing itself is not by any means the whole story, and in order that it be perfectly intelligible all questions and remarks interjected by the sitter must also be accurately recorded. Nor is this all. The story is not then complete unless one knows how to make notes of and interpret more or less correctly the various and significant gestures of the hand, which appears to be sensitive and alive, as if an actual intelligence were seated in it. Therefore I cannot see why, either at a voice sitting or at a writing sitting, much has not to be trusted to the person who does the recording, although still more perhaps must be trusted to the person who does the interpreting, in cases where recorder and interpreter do not happen to be one.

I have a great mass of communications extending through the years, and can only publish extracts from them. I have decided that it is best to confine these extracts almost entirely to communications from one personality, giving continuous talk, which in a voice sitting has much fewer breaks than occur in the writing.

There is not in my case, as exists in many cases, any special reason why I should withhold the identity of the one who has been my special communicator of recent years, namely, Augustus Pearl Martin. In fact, it is for the very reason that he was widely known in both public and private life in the city of Boston that I am speaking openly and freely, and offering communications which purport to have come from him since his passing out in 1902. I am also desirous of making my offering without further delay, and before his strong personality shall have become dim in the memory of his large acquaintance. I am hoping thereby to interest people in my subject who as yet know little about it, or who have hitherto taken no special interest in it.

I do not consider that I have any right to publish this name, however, against the wishes or without the express consent of the nearest surviving relatives. This consent I have obtained, as will appear in the following copy of a letter written by the widow and endorsed by the son.

769 Morton St., Dorchester, Mass.,
May 10, 1908.

My Dear Miss Robbins: I have no objection to your publishing the name of my late husband in connection with your work with Mrs. Piper, if you choose to do so. I appreciate the great assistance you rendered him during the last years of his life, and can assure you that his friendly feeling for you was shared not only by myself but by all the members of my family. I have known of your long-continued interest in psychical research, and if he were here to-day I am sure he would trust your judgment in any matter of this kind. I would prefer not to have details concerning myself or my family published, but otherwise you are at liberty to use the name as you see fit.

Yours sincerely,

ABBIE F. MARTIN.

I most heartily endorse the above.

EVERETT F. MARTIN.

There have been anxious inquiries and loving messages for members of his own family, but most of these I must omit. Many references to other persons also, friends and relatives of my own, must be omitted.

Where there is a decided change in the subject of the running talk, if it is something that must be omitted I have indicated the omission by dotted lines. Omissions of single words or brief phrases, which do not in the least affect the sense, some of which are made merely to avoid repetition, I have not indicated and must ask the reader to place confidence in the discretion I have tried to exercise on these points. Some personal references must be omitted in any case, and one object for adopting the method of abbreviating here indicated is to make the record more readable. The technical report of the automatic writing, with all its confusions, breaks and undecipherable scrawls, is fascinating reading for the student, but is often, by reason of its unintelligible technicality, unattractive to the average reader.

Further than this it is only necessary for the uninitiated to remember that all remarks enclosed in round brackets are my own. All remarks enclosed in square brackets are not a part of the sitting but simply my explanatory notes. All of the remainder of the record represents what is said by the communicating spirit.

It hardly seems necessary for me to make the statement here and at this late day that the possibility of Mrs. Piper's seeking information in a normal way to give out in her trance was years ago entirely dropped from the consideration of her case by those familiar with it. She of course must be more or less familiar with the names of men who have been in the public eye. She had only the very slightest personal acquaintance with my communicator when he was living, never having met him more than once or twice and then only casually. She has never seen one of my reports, nor had she any idea up to within a few months of date of publication that I intended to publish, at which time I obtained her full consent to publishing whatever relates to her in this volume.

XI
EXTRACTS FROM REPORTS OF SITTINGS

SITTING OF DECEMBER 23, 1903

Rector controlling

Art thou here? Art thou present?

(I am.)

In God's holy name we greet thee this day and this hour. We sent for thee to return to us that we might make all clear to thee, bring messages from those who seek thee on our side and teach thee the divine and holy will of God. Hearest thou me?

(I do. I am glad I have not been dropped from the fold.)

Dropped, friend? Not one lamb who cometh unto us, who seeketh us in the highest, who have faith in God, will depart from us or will we allow them to drift from the fold unprotected or unguided. Thy friends on this side hath sought thee often.

(Friend?)

Friends. They have sought thee, they have called us to seek thee, to find thee out, to bring thee unto us and unto them. Hearest thou me?

(Yes.)

Friend, oh those of little faith know not the workings of the Allwise. . . . I am Rector, servant of God. I bring to thee first thy friend known as Hiram.

[My old friend of early sittings, who passed away in 1885, known in old reports as "H." There was some talk here which I understood to be by Hiram Hart, but, while in the earlier years he talked very naturally, his style being very unlike that of Rector, at this time the two personalities were so much alike that I could not clearly distinguish when one left off speaking and the other began. It appeared later, however, that Rector brought Hiram Hart, and the latter came to introduce the friend who had never before made his appearance. For he said:]

I am bringing another friend who seeks you, who knows you as you are. He would speak also, but the awakening of his soul was the most remarkable I have ever known. I sought him and found him. He sought me. We found each other. We are together. We clasp hands, we are friends.

(Yes.)

They call him on our side "General."

(I see.)

I know not his other name so well, but he is known by this and we call him this, and he is happy but longs to meet you. Do you hear?

(Yes.)

. . . .

Now here comes the General. Will you speak to him?

(Oh, I should be delighted.)

[What immediately follows I understood to be the first words that came from the later acquaintance, who passed out about twenty-one months previous to date of this sitting.]

The General

I want to see you. I want everything to be understood between us, and until it is I do not feel satisfied. Can't you help me? Can't you see the obstacles in my way?

[A few brief phrases only omitted here.]

Can't you see that God's will was better? Oh, you are not so weak as I thought in your belief. Why didn't I know better? Well, because I was grappling with the world. That is it.

(Is this Hiram talking, or is he talking for the General?)

No, he is talking for the General. He is quoting the General's words. You remember the little poem,

> Tell me, ye winged winds
>   That round my pathway roar,
> Do ye not know some spot —

[Words not all correctly caught here, but

these are the first lines of the verse he was trying to quote.]

You remember that?

(Yes.)

You remember,

> Some lone and pleasant dell,
> Some valley in the West,
> Where free from toil and pain,
> The weary soul may rest?

(General, you used to repeat a lot of poetry, didn't you?)

Oh, I forgot,— yes, I did. I have found that peace, that rest, the beautiful awakening of the spirit.

. . . . . .

I have longed for a talk with you, but I did not understand the conditions.

(Yes, I have been only waiting patiently for you to come.)

You have called for me in your spirit. I knew it and felt it, but I could not reach down until the conditions were arranged for it. Do you know what they all mean? Perhaps you know better than I do. But these good priests [who] opened the way, who showed me the Light, opened the door for me and here I am. Would to God you could see me as I am! I am quite the man that I was, only my ideas are all changed. They are more now I think in harmony with your own. . . .

Oh, it is beautiful, it is ideal, just over the river, lift the Veil and you know all. Tell me something of yourself.

. . . . . .

But oh, why was I so blind? It was because of the thickness, the thickness of the flesh.

(General, do you know what I am doing?)

Yes, I know it well. Do you mean the nature of the work, or the private work?

(I mean this minute.)

This present minute?

(Yes.)

Why, aren't you registering something?

(Yes.)

I can see your hand move and I can see your spirit, too, so plainly, and the spiritual hand guides the material hand, and it seems as though it was registering something. Is it what I am saying?

(Yes.)

Well, that is natural.

(Well, I guess so.)

That is natural, and how rapidly you worked with that for me. I shall never forget those days.

[This of course refers to the eight years of association in public office, and especially to the first five, when I reported hearings, conferences, etc., at which he presided, and also wrote much at his dictation.]

And do you remember the last time I saw you in the body?

(Yes.)

You remember what you said to me? Do you remember saying "I think you are getting better?"

(I think I said that, that time.)

[I said this many times to him during his illness, and probably said it the last time I saw him.]

Yes, you did. You were so hopeful and you helped me so much, but I could not tell you all I felt. Do you hear?

(Yes.)

[It was generally understood among those who were near him that my hope for his recovery was stronger than that of any one else, though no one else knew the ground for my hope. Strong prophetic statements had been made to me, regarding future work, etc., which involved his life, and which, it seemed to me then, could not possibly reach their fulfilment if he died.]

. . . . . .

Can't you speak to me and tell me something of yourself?

(I will speak slowly so that I can register it.)

["Register" is a term used from the Other Side, which I adopted.]

All right. Do you remember coming to me

and telling me about your belief, and do you remember I said I would like to accept it, but I did not know, I did not understand?

(I knew that was the way you felt.)

But I felt that all through. I could not understand it. I do now. What fools we are! But those few who seek light and light is given them are blest, aren't they?

(General, do you remember the very last words that you said to me?)

The last words that I said were — I think I said — didn't I say I should see you again and ask you to come out?

["To come out" is exactly the right expression. His home was in the suburbs of Boston, about six miles from the centre.]

(Well, you expected me out the next day.)

Oh, I said good bye to you. I said "good bye, come to-morrow," "I shall see you to-morrow," or something — I can't remember the exact words, but that is the idea. What were they?

(The very last words that you said were "good night." You said that just as [naturally] as though you were perfectly well.)

Yes, I remember saying good bye to you. I remember thinking, looking forward to see you again. Then what was the next thing? Then I passed over —

(Yes.)

— between that time and the time you —

did *not* come again. Tell me a little about that. That may help me to come.

(Do you remember you used to sit in a chair?)

Oh, yes. I remember one thing, I remember sitting with a blanket over my knees, over my body.

[He sat that way nearly all the time day and night for a year, not being able to lie down during the greater part of his illness, and he was rarely without a blanket over his knees, even in the warmest weather.]

[There is a little further talk here about the conditions of his illness.]

(General, do you remember —)

How far away are you now from here? You seem quite a little distance away.

[I had not been quite close to the psychic. I moved a little nearer and put my hand on her shoulder.]

(My hand is on the medium's shoulder.)

I suppose it is because the flesh divides us.

(Do you remember that I used to bring messages through this same channel?)

Oh, I remember there was a friend of yours, a lady in the body — now who was she? I can't think what her name was, but she lived somewhere in some other town, and you used to go and see her and then come and bring me messages from the priests who are helping me now. But I can't remember who she was, but I remember the messages perfectly, the nature of the messages, and they really helped me. They gave me great encouragement, and that is all I needed, was encouragement, until time helped me over.

[Arlington Heights, where Mrs. Piper then lived, is about eight miles from Boston centre in an opposite direction from where his home was.]

What was you going to say about the messages? Oh I wish you knew how I felt, how light I am, how I can see, how I can read and how I can move about, how free I am from encumbrance, how clear my mind is, how really supremely happy I am. You would be delighted for my sake.

(I never wanted to call you back.)

Good! You knew too well how I suffered. But tell me about the children. I would like to know a little something about the children.

[There is quite a little conversation here about members of his own family about whom he seemed eager to hear, and he asked if I had been out to his home since he passed away.]

[About six months after the General died a grandson about two years of age, who was named for him, passed away. Another grandson was born on Dec. 16, 1903, just a week previous to date of the present sitting. I knew only of the fact, did not know what the child was named, or whether it was named at all. But in giving him information about the family into which this child was born, I say, referring to the father of the child:]

(And he has got a new baby. Did you know that?)

Yes, the little one I knew about. . . . It is just the little details of the material life which I cannot grasp and [in] which I long to have you help me, but the actual life, and the actual life of the children, and all that, is well known to me, but the details of the material life I cannot see.

(Do you remember little Augustus?)

Oh, yes. Tell me about him.

(Do you know where he is?)

Well, I know about the little one that came over. I know him. He is with me and we are very happy together. But didn't he name the other —

(I don't know what he has named him yet.)

Hasn't he called him Augustus? He has, I am sure, one of the two names. But his first one is with me.

(Now I don't know whether he has named him Augustus or not —)

Well, he has.

(— so that will be a good test for me.)

That is one of his names.

(I will find out about it.)

And sometime you can speak with me about it, but meanwhile I know it is true. But the little fellow followed me very soon, didn't he?

(Yes.)

I knew, and I was so glad to have him come, and he is better off here, much better off. In fact, it is all right. I have no words of complaint to offer.

[I ascertained afterwards that the new baby was named William Everett, but his mother told me that they *called* him Augustus nearly all the time. He seemed to take the place of the little Augustus whom they lost.]

. . . . . .

Are you getting along all right in the world?

[I do not reply immediately.]

(You know I want to take this all down, and that is why I am a little slow.)

Oh, I see. Well, don't hurry. There is no hurry in this world. I see a light burning, and at the end of that light I am talking, and when the light begins to go out, of course I must go. That is, I can't talk with you, but I shall be with you just the same and you will be conscious of it. Are you getting along as well as when I was with you?

(Oh, about as well.)

Do you have to work hard?

(Well, I have to work every day.)

But not any harder?

(No.)

I am glad. I would like to see you a little free for a few hours in what we used to call day, and have a little leisure for rest and reading up on subjects concerning the advancements of a higher life, and it would be so much better if you could, so much more helpful. And yet the body has to be fed, I know. It has to be clothed. I know that and don't forget those things in my experience, but still there is a great deal beside that. That is nothing, that is only the covering.

(Well, I have been told that I should be free some time, but I do not see much prospect of it now.)

Yes, I do. I see all round you light, which indicates more rest, less hard work, and that is the reason why I spoke to you,— if it was not very near you. It must be, I can see it so plainly.

. . . . . .

Will you tell me now if you are really having any rest?

(A little in the evening, that is all.)

Work all day?

(Yes.)

Isn't it daytime with you now?

(I got off. I got excused.)

But that is something new for you.

(Well, I managed it.)

I mean, it isn't a thing that you — you used to stick pretty well.

(I would not get off for anything but you, to come and see you. I would give up everything for that.)

Oh, yes. Are you really physically well?

(I am quite well, and trying to be very well.)

[I mention some slight physical ailment.]

Well, don't you know you must be out in the air a great deal. You must go what we used to call walking, and be out in the air a great deal, too. You can get out. Don't confine yourself to the four walls of your room. Now that is my advice. Can't you go up to the library? You remember the library. Go up there and get a little reading matter. Take the walk to and fro. Go back and read a little, take in a little study. That will help us in the work and that is all you need to do. Eat slowly. Don't hurry so. Take plenty of time and be careful what you do eat. That is my advice to you. I am a little weak just now and my thoughts begin to tremble.

(Are you speaking through the medium, or is Hiram interpreting for you now?)

Hiram is doing it for me. I could not take possession of the medium yet.

(Can you do it some time?)

Yes, but not just now. I am trying to understand the laws and the workings of the machine, and they put me up here so I could see. Just like a schoolboy being sent to the board to figure out a multiplication table. I am set up here, I am held here, and there are three clergymen, one behind me and one on either side of me, holding me up here and telling me to talk, and I am talking to Hiram, and Hiram is repeating it after me, and I am trying to do a sum in geometry. That is just what I am trying to do. And since I am not fully equipped in that problem perhaps you can understand something of the difficulty.

(I think you are doing wonderfully well.)

But I can hear you, and so long as I can hear you and get my thoughts over the line clear, that is all I want.

(General, as far as I have heard, you have done wonderfully well for the first time.)

They have been preparing me for months and months to make me understand it. They have put me up here and taken me away again. They have held me up and showed me the Light, and said, "do this and do that, and see this and see that," and shown me the details, and the ins and outs and the whys and wherefores, and why shouldn't I learn something after having it hammered into me all that time. Then I said, well, I must reach her. It is an utter impossibility for me to [let go?] until I do. [I will] move heaven and earth, but I must reach her. And they said:

"Wait, you have got to learn. You must go here with us, you must stand on this side, hold up your hands, bow your head, speak in this kind of a way, speak slowly, articulate distinctly,"— but without the preparation there is a good deal of confusion. But they are very, very good to me, and they know — what they don't know about the details of this Light is not worth knowing, I assure you that, if you can grasp me. With your clear mind you can grasp it pretty well, I think.

[There is some talk about the private work and he expresses himself very emphatically.]

(General, you are just as positive as you used to be, aren't you?)

[The psychic seemed to smile.]

Perhaps you would not recognize me if I was not. Well, I have retained my individuality, thank God. Do you know where Poland is, Poland [hesitating only a moment] Springs?

(Oh, I guess I do.)

Do you remember about it?

(Yes, indeed.)

Well, I don't think anybody except ourselves —

(Why, they know where it is, of course.)

But I mean I had an interest in it. I mean I loved it.

(I know you loved it much.)

You might go there some time. You

know it came into my mind as soon as could be.

[The place where the famous Poland Spring is located is the one spot on earth that he loved. He was born about three miles from the hill on which the large hotel now stands. He was always supplied with the water and thought it the finest water in the world. There was no thought of the place in my mind when he made reference to it.]

Here is little Augustus. Don't you see him?

(Is he here?)

Yes, as happy as a bee, just as busy. He is a dear little fellow.

(Give him my love if he understands it.)

Well, I will. He will be glad to have it. Do you remember rubbing my arms?

(Yes.)

Well, they don't need rubbing any more, thank God.

Now before I get too weak — you know this is quite an effort for me for the first time — before my thoughts begin to wander, have you got any especial question you wish to ask me about my life, about anything —

(Well, General, I want you to try and think up some of the details of the last moments, or rather, after you passed out, the first few days.)

[I referred to details of what happened

with me, or at his home, but my question is not clear.]

I know what it was. When I first passed out my mind was cloudy, rather confused. I felt as though I was going into space, did not know where, drifting as it were, for a few hours — that was all — and then I felt as though there was a strong hand grasped me and said to me: "It is all right, it is all over." And I said: "What is over?" I could not seem to understand what it all meant, and after a little while, perhaps an hour, possibly an hour or two, I saw oh such a light! You cannot imagine it, cannot conceive what it is like. It is the most brilliant and yet the softest moonlight that you ever saw, and I thought, what a beautiful light it was! And all of a sudden I saw people moving about. I saw their heads, their figures. Then they seemed all clad in white, and I could not seem to make them out. They were moving in the air.

And I said: "What is this place? Where am I? What am I? What has happened?" It was all such a puzzle to me. When I get strong I will tell you about it. I can't tell you any more. Now what you want me to do, think over the few days —

(Before I come again, I mean.)

— and when I come back, to tell you what my experience was. I tell you one thing, the clergyman who is talking for me now was the best friend I ever had, and he said: "Come along, it is all right, I will show you the way; it is all right, you will get over this confusion in a minute, and I will help you." And I said: "Who are you? What are you? What are you here for? Where am I? Where am I going? What am I doing? What does all this mean?" He said: "Never mind, it will all be clear to you in a few minutes. Just wait patiently and come with me." And he stood ready to welcome me.

(Well, who was he?)

Well, his name is Hart.

(Oh!)

He says: "I know who you know, you know who I know, now we will be friends together, and this is all right; I have had experience and I know, and I will explain it to you in a few minutes." I thought I saw the doctor bending over me and I wanted him to get away. He seemed to be in my way as I was going out. I wanted to get away from him, and all of a sudden I was going through this misty, cloudy way, and then I went past [possibly "fast," word not caught] until I got to this light, and it was like going up, up, up in the air, in a balloon as it were. You could not conceive of anything more strange and beautiful, in a sense — the confusion was not so beautiful, but because it was so I could not seem to retain my consciousness and could not seem to be released from the burden that hung over me, and all of a sudden, the moment I realized that this hand was on my arm, then I began to see clearly; and from that moment I have been advancing and going on, and I have seen everybody I ever knew, and I have had the happiest time you could imagine. I have a mansion all my own and live in it just the same as you live in your place there, just the same. I have walls, I have pictures, I have music, I have books, I have poetry, I have *everything*.

(I see.)

It is not a *fac simile* of that life, but that life is a miserable shadow of what this really is, and when I get strong, as I become stronger, and,— that is, more accustomed to using this line, I can tell you more clearly about it.

Well, it has been, oh, I can't tell you what it means to me to see you. I can't tell you how you have cleared my mind. I can't tell you what you have done for me. Now I am going to repay it all back by turning and working for you.

[It was early morning when the General died. His doctor was not present. Two of his sons were present and must have been bending over him, for as they were helping him back into his chair which he had left for a few moments his strength gave way entirely and he passed out shortly after.

Hiram Hart was not a clergyman in this life, but he came in time to be spoken of at the sittings as such and I was told that he had become one. Although he passed out nine years before I became acquainted with the General, he seems to have been the latter's guide through the misty passage that separates the two worlds.]

. . . .

I think I shall have to go. How long have I been here?

(Nearly an hour.)

An hour in the earthly world? Well, I don't know how long that is, but I am too weak to remain; that is, I am afraid I can't use this Light any more.

[A few words of farewell. Then, in a most natural, persuasive tone, as if addressing a child:]

Come, Augustus, you come with me, dear, and we will go and find some play toys. We will have a good time together. Come with grandpa, come along.

[Then as if addressing me:]

He is going.

Rector returns

It is I, Rector.

(I am glad to see you, Rector.)

I have returned, friend, because our Leader said to me to keep the passageway clear and keep all right. Friend, all is right in thy world with us this day. Thou hast good conditions for us. Art thou aware of it?

(I am glad to know that.)

[I had a long talk with Rector, during which I asked:]

(Is the General coming here much through this medium?)

At times he is. He is a marvelous personality and he has a very clear mind, and he has a very earnest desire to work for God and humanity.

[It must be remembered that the spirit known as "Rector," the so-called "control," always appears at the opening of a sitting and again at its close. Sometimes there are long conversations with him, much spiritual advice and help is given, and quite often messages for other persons are received by the sitter, or messages from other persons are delivered by the sitter to the trance personalities.]

Close

SITTING OF MAY 24, 1904

[Soon after the opening of this sitting Rector introduced to me a personality purporting to be a physician, who held a long conversation with me in regard to my health. He told me that he formerly lived in Boston, that he was in Paris when he passed out, that he had been gone possibly a year or two. I afterwards ascertained that a physician by the name given, one with which I was not familiar, had lived on Beacon St., Boston, and died in Paris early in the preceding September. This explains reference to "the doctor" in opening remarks below.]

The General

[Psychic coughing]

Well, I wonder if there is anybody wishes to see me!

(Hiram?)

No, my name is Martin. I want to see Miss Robbins. Is she present?

(Is this you, General?)

It is . . . I am delighted to see you, that goes without saying. Well, how are you?

(Oh, I am pretty well.)

You look splendidly. I saw the doctor, I met him. As I came in he was just going out. By the way, I want to give you a bit of advice. Whatever you do in that world, don't overdo. You know I was a great one to preach.

(Well, no, I don't think you were.)

Well, that makes me laugh. You know I don't think I did preach very much, but I am going to preach now. I am going to tell you to take care of yourself and the Lord will take care of you. What are you doing?

(Now I want to take down every word that you say and what I say.)

Well, you can do it, you are equal to it. I will try to be as slow as I can. Well, are you pretty well?

(Yes, pretty well, I am going to be better.)

You want to get some of these friends over here after you. I have been studying into this thing, studying the laws of our nature — that is, its problems on our side — and I am perfectly delighted with the conditions. I am perfectly delighted with the thought of returning. I seek you out and follow you night and day. I am often standing by your side when you don't realize it, and I stand there and laugh at myself to see how utterly unconcerned you are in regard to my presence, but I say but if her spiritual eyes could open and she could see me as I am I know she would be delighted. By the way, haven't you a sister?

(Yes.)

She has just passed through some sorrow in the earthly world?

(Yes.)

What has been her sorrow, her loss, has been somebody else's gain. Because she had, well, I think it is a husband — . . .

[I have a sister whose husband passed out in the early part of this year, only a few months previously. I have other sisters, but do not live with any of them. This particular sister had just been spending some months with me. My communicator had met her once or twice only in life, and was not at all well acquainted.]

[I think I asked at this point if he was talking through Rector, my question not being recorded.]

Oh, Rector is holding the Light. I could not, they would not allow me to do that. Not quite now, but I may be able to later. But they have to support the Light, some friend has to look after it.

(Do you want me to tell you a few things, just the same as if you were here?)

Just the same. How is Everett, by the way?

[Everett is one of his sons, now living.]

(Everett is well. I saw him a few days ago and took supper with him and his family —)

[Interrupting]

I know it. I know about the children. You know there is a little one over here. We are very friendly with each other, and just as near to each other as we ever could be.

[There is more talk about his son, and I ask:]

(When do you think it would be well to send a message to him?)

I think it would be perfectly safe to do it, — well, we will say in a few months.

[Further talk on same line]

Don't you remember the talks we used to have together about this thing? And then I was a little skeptical, I could not seem to take it in. But I have taken it in to my satisfaction.

[I relate to him a story of something that transpired during his last illness, of which he was entirely ignorant, something which involved a reference to a number of his old friends, most of them well known public men.]

(Do you think you would remember any of the names if I should mention them?)

I think I should. Many names have gone from me, naturally, and new ones have come up to me. Names of places, names of people whom I knew in the mortal world, have gone from me to a certain extent, and as I go on they go still farther from me, but I shall never forget you. I remember when I was suffering so, I remember the little councils we had together, and they have lasted in my memory and will to the end of all life.

(General, it seems to be the real spiritual sympathies that you remember only —)

Yes, well, those are the vital ones, those are the real ones. And when you understand better the conditions of life and the conditions of passing from that life to this, the changes in the life as it were, you will understand more clearly what that means. But until then it will be difficult for you to understand it fully. I have got to go out a moment — you will excuse me — I must go for a little change. My thoughts begin to wander, and if I stayed you would be displeased with my wandering thoughts, so I will just go out and get refreshed and return instantly.

[Silence for perhaps a minute, possibly not as long]

Are you still here?

(Yes.)

I feel better now. I want to know about the help to my family. What help have they now?

[Some talk about family omitted.]

(You remember that you thought you knew the name of the new baby, and you said it was Augustus; well, it was not Augustus, but the mother told me that they *called* him Augustus nearly all the time —)

Yes, that is what led me — what is his name?

(It is William Everett. They call him Augustus when they speak about him.)

I heard it so much I felt sure it was his name. Now I want to know how you are getting on and what you think about our writing that book.

[Immediately reverts to family again.]

(General, shall I tell you one or two more things before you speak of the book?)

Yes, you might.

(There was a man in the State's prison — you know — you used to see him sometimes with your old friend Chase —)

Oh yes!

(— and when you passed away he found it out and got together a dollar or two and gave it to some one and asked him if he would buy a rosebush and put it on your grave. I wrote him a letter after that about it, and now he is out of prison, and he came to see me to thank me for the letter and express his admiration and love for you.)

That is very beautiful, very beautiful. I am very glad to hear that. Who was he?

(Oh, he was some old burglar or something, nobody that you cared anything about —)

[I apologize to-day, 1909, to whom it may concern, for this thoughtless reply.]

But had a heart?

(Yes, had a heart. Now do you remember how you used to lecture on Gettysburg?)

Oh, yes, I do, yes I do very well.

(Well, after you went away I got your speeches and put them together and made a nice good complete copy, as well as I could, and your wife has one of them and I have one.

Did you know anything about it when I was doing it?)

Well, yes, I knew the outline, but the work itself, the actual work as it was going on, I could not fathom. But I knew the work concerned my mortal life and things that transpired in it. But the nature of it I could not define. We know generally what takes place in a general way, but if we were to define it, condense it and give utterance to it, it would be difficult. But such is the law of this life.

Remember, now, if you could see me you would say I was a mere film, and you would say, 'how transparent and peculiar and how light and how strange you look to me;' and you would say, 'where is your body? you look like a shadow, as it were,' but still I could talk with you, we could converse with each other, and you would be surprised to see how real I am. The passing out is really beautiful, just after you once get beyond the border, it is perfectly beautiful. You know the meaning of the word heaven? Well, it is heaven indeed. But the coming back is a little confusing at first and we have to learn.

(I think you are good to come back from such a place.)

Well, I have attractions and you seek for me and I find you. Don't get nervous, keep calm, we shall have time to say all there is to say.

(Did you know anything about your funeral at the time?)

Yes, I knew it and saw the body and saw the flowers. I saw the way in which it was laid out. I saw — don't you think it looked well? I looked as though I was asleep, don't you think so? And I don't think the face showed suffering — that is, the clay did not show the suffering, the body itself — but I felt, oh, I was so pleased to be out and away from the atmosphere, I felt so choked and so distressed for breath, and the moment I was released from the imprisoning body then I could breathe perfectly. I felt,— I could not describe it to you.

(Well, you had a beautiful funeral and a large one, and do you remember your old friend Horton, the minister?

[Rev. Edward A. Horton, who conducted the funeral service. They were familiar friends.]

Yes, yes, very well.

(I wrote him and thanked him for all he said, and thanked him for you, too. Was that right?)

Beautiful, that is beautiful! What did he say?

(Oh, he wrote me a very nice letter, and he said if I was satisfied he thought it must have been satisfactory to others, because I was so close to you and knew you so well.)

That is beautiful. I can only say to that, Amen.

[Only one or two remarks of a personal nature omitted here.]

(Now I will let you say what you want to.)

I want to say this, that when you are working I sometimes dictate thoughts to you, and it is surprising to me to see how clearly you register them, and I think sometimes you are surprised to think that you have done what you have, and if you just stop and give me a thought you would know why it was that you did those things, registered those thoughts. Sometimes there seems to be a barrier between you and your thoughts, they are not clear, and they seem to be a little obscure, and then they clear up [marvelously], and you have always attributed that to the condition of your own brain, and now if you just give me credit for a little bit of help you would do the right thing. Not that I am egotistic, but the point is that I am really with you. And I want to say one thing, that you have not grown old in spirit and not in the flesh. It looks so clear to me, so free, so bright and so young, and I think your body looks the same. I can't see much change. Yes, I think you look about the same. I can't see the body so clearly as I can the spirit.

(Do you know how old I am?)

[A brief talk about age omitted. He

thought me older than I then was. It was evidently the comparison of ages which carried him back to old associations, for he immediately followed it by saying:]

You remember how we used to talk in the office there? Where is that office now? Is it there? Is the building gone away?

[Referring, I presume, to the office of the Board of Police in Pemberton square.]

(Not that I know of. You mean where we were so long together?)

They are going to remove it and put another in its place.

[This matter was talked of as long ago as when he was there, and I think he had plans in his own mind for a new building. The particular building in which the old office was located has not yet (1909) been replaced by a new one, although new large buildings have recently gone up close beside it.]

(They had to get another lady there, couldn't get along without the ladies.)

I know they did. That is very funny. Do you ever see anything of Hanscom?

(Oh, why yes,— I don't see him often, but he has a good place there and is well and comfortable. I am so pleased that you should think of his name.)

I could not help thinking about him. All of a sudden I thought of him, and I have seen him several times since I passed over. I have seen him discussing something there with another man in the office, and my mind reverted back to the office and the conditions until I happened to think of him. He was not well at one time, but he is better now — that is, since I passed over.

(Perhaps you like him better than you used to?)

Because I see his principles.

(I don't believe you quite understood him.)

I didn't.

(But I did better than you did.)

Yes, . . . but I did not understand what his active principles were. If you have an opportunity I wish in an indirect way, if not direct, I wish you could mention me to him, will you? Tell him that you have met me.

(Perhaps I might have him call on me, but I don't want to give too much of you away, you are too precious, but I think he would be pleased to hear what you have said about him.)

Well, tell him that I appreciate all his efforts and everything that he did a great deal better perhaps now than ever. And I would like to have you tell him that for me. I don't want people to think that you are losing your mind, but I think you are far more capable of keeping your mind by finding me perhaps than others, than some of those who perhaps would not listen to it. So we will keep that a secret between ourselves.

(You better leave that to my discretion, about seeing him.)

I will.

[Orinton M. Hanscom was formerly one of the higher officials in the police department. In 1888, after a protracted hearing on charges preferred against him, and a decided disagreement among the members of the board in regard to the case, he was discharged from the force. I have memoranda in shorthand under date of December, 1888, to the effect that Dr. Phinuit, the early control of Mrs. Piper, predicted to me that Mr. Hanscom would sometime go back to his old position. In March, 1889, the prediction was repeated, that he would go back to his old position or to his old surroundings. He was out of the department six years. In 1894, after General Martin became chairman of the board, his case was reopened and he was reinstated in the department, being appointed to a higher position than the one he formerly occupied, namely, that of deputy-superintendent. There had formerly never been more than one deputy-superintendent, but now two more men were given that ranking, Mr. Hanscom being one of them. The General, therefore, had shown himself very friendly to Mr. Hanscom, but when, after the reinstatement, they came to be actively associated, I think there was a feeling of disappointment on the part of the General in Mr. Hanscom. The latter was a man of rather broad outlook, with ideas of reform, which he liked to discuss, but his ideas did not always seem to be appreciated by his fellows or superiors. The General wanted his orders put into effect quickly, even though they might be difficult of execution. There was, therefore, this lack of harmony between the two men, which was perfectly apparent to me at the time. Therefore the remarks of my communicator given above, to the effect that he did not understand his active principles, but that he appreciated all his efforts now better than he ever did before, wishing to be remembered to Mr. Hanscom, are extremely pertinent. Some time after date of this sitting I met Mr. Hanscom accidentally and gave him the substance of the message, which he received with the courtesy habitual to him, refraining from criticism. Since then he has himself passed away. [1]]

[1] Since the above was written Mr. Hanscom has purported to return. This occurred at a sitting which took place on Dec. 16, 1908. The communications were suddenly broken off and I was told that a friend wanted to speak to me. I had no thought of any one but Hiram Hart, who I presumed was interrupting for a word of greeting. Rector stumbled a little over the name, but only a little, calling it "Hanson." Not till that moment did the thought of Hanscom enter my mind. I asked Rector to get the name exactly, and he spelled it out easily and correctly: "H a n s c o m — Orin. Don't

[In conversation about my private work, where it would be best to spend my vacation, etc., I say:]

(Greenacre,— don't you remember I used to go there?)

I should approve of that at once, and sanction it.

[Reference to Greenacre will appear in a later sitting.]

Do you remember a woman you used to talk to me about in the body who used to have,— the spirits used to speak through her?

(Yes.)

[This refers, of course, to Mrs. Piper.]

Well, I want you some time to be in her surrounding when I am not speaking and see if I can reach you, see if the thoughts will be clearer to you. I think it would be worth while to try it, because I often reach over the line when I don't speak.

(Do you mean when the Light is not working?)

you remember Orin?" It did not occur to me until after the sitting that the Christian name should have been "Orinton" and not "Orin." I do not know whether his intimate friends called him "Orin" when in life or not, but it is quite likely they did. There was a very brief conversation. He said: "What a happy ending to a blighted career!" Mrs. Piper, in her normal state, faintly recalled the name as that of some one whom she had heard spoken of, but said she did not know that he had passed to the Other Side. His death occurred in November, 1907.

When the Light is not working, when it is closed.

(We were together a while ago in an evening, but then there were a good many people about.)

I mean quietly, when there is nobody about except the spiritual intelligences and when we are not actually acting upon it, and I think ideas would come to you very clearly.

[I cannot say that any special experiment on my part was made in accordance with this request. Opportunities to be with Mrs. Piper alone, when not in trance, were rare with me.]

I have got to go out to get my breath. I will be right back in a moment, but I have to refresh myself.

[While the General is apparently *out,* Hiram Hart steps in, speaking hurriedly as if he had only a moment, and saying that he saw the other gentleman "going out," so thought he would "come in" and say "how do you do." As he appears to be going I say: "Oh, have you got to go?" He replies: "Oh, they have kept him so clear I want him to learn what I know." The other gentleman then returns.]

Well, I am right back here again. I met Mr. Hart and he told me he just wanted to speak to you a moment while I was refreshing myself, so I said "go ahead and ask Rector if you can get in." Wasn't he a clergyman?

(He was not here, but he says he is now.)

Well, he is preaching and praying and helping all the people that come over this side — or the spirits — and he is a wonderful preacher and he has done a great deal for me, and I am glad to know him because he was your friend. They say it is not all gold that glitters, but there is a great deal glitters here that is gold.

(Well, he seems to admire you. He says you are very handsome.)

[Laughing]

Well, I suppose he thinks so.

(You used to be here.)

Oh, you think so? There is no accounting for tastes, you know. But we have to accept those things. He is a good soul and I like him. He has done, I say, a great deal for me, pointed out the way a great many times.

(Now, General, I will let you say what you want to, but you were going to tell me something,— what happened just after you went out, either on this side or on your side. Give me some new ideas, will you?)

Yes, I will. You know the actual passing out of the body, there is a little feeling of, sort of depression, as it were, and then when I passed out, just as I passed out, I began to feel uplifted. I felt as though the air was filled with perfume, and I was [soaring], rising, rising, rising above my body until I passed behind simply a veil. It is thin. It blinds your vision. It obstructs the vision for a moment from the earthly world. Then after we have passed beyond it, why the music, the flowers, the trees, the birds, the lakes, the rivers, the hills, the gardens, the walks, are *perfectly magnificent, perfectly magnificent,* and nothing in the earthly world hardly can even correspond to them. And we are taken up by perhaps a priest, or man that acts in the capacity of what you would understand as a clergyman, and they say: "This is a state of transition. You are now in the real life, in the new life. You will not see the face of the Father for many, many years, but He will give you strength and power to go back if you wish and see those whom you have left behind." And the feeling of ecstasy is beyond description, and no spirit that ever returned to earth could begin to describe it for the understanding of the mortal mind.

And then I was surrounded by friends, by acquaintances, by old war veterans, by my intimate friends whom I know, members of my family and all, surrounded by them, welcoming me. Why, I felt as though I should be enveloped by them, the delight was so great, but when I tried to call them by name I was at a loss to do so. They had to tell me who they were. I knew their faces, not one failed to me. I knew them and understood them well. I saw them and recognized them, but to call them by name, believe me, I could not. And when I tried to speak I found instead of it being an effort and difficult for me to speak, I found that my thoughts were understood, actually understood, and their thoughts were returned to me. There was a perfect communion between us.

And then I was taken — would you believe it if I should tell you? I was taken to an actual mansion. It would be what you would call a palace. There is a garden, walks about it. It is divided into rooms, actual compartments. I was taken to that and [they] said: "Here is your home; occupy it, live in it; have what friends you choose with you, what relatives you choose with you, and as those whom you have left behind follow you, you may welcome them to this home as you may see fit." Do you understand it?

(Yes.)

I went in and looked about me. I said: "Where does this music come from?" I walked through a corridor and turned into a room at the right and actually walked without fatigue, without effort; I simply glided in. I saw beautiful pictures upon the walls, I saw beautiful flowers that we called in the body palms, growing about me. I heard this beautiful music. I stepped along to a window and looked out, and under the window there were fifty young, beautiful faces, all playing,— an orchestra. That was my welcome, that was my serenade, as it were. And they said: "This is heaven, this is the spiritual world. We greet you." I went to the window and as I looked out upon the orchestra they each one bowed and waved their hands, and yet the music continued. They were playing upon instruments, actual instruments, all in harmony, and I never heard anything like it in the earthly world. The music was divine. I said: "I would like to go elsewhere." I bade them good-bye, as it were,— I just saluted them and passed along across the corridor back through the room, across the corridor into the opposite side.

I said: "Now I would like to see if it is possible, I would like to see flowers about me." I went to the window, and would you believe, the flowers appeared to me in masses, *en masse,* I might say, and I never saw such flowers. There were lilies, roses, violets, geraniums, carnations, azaleas, hyacinths, tulips, poppies, of every conceivable description, not all intermingled, but each one in its own place. What could you find, what could one wish for better than that?

I said: "Now if it is wise and right that I should seek it, I would like to hear something that sounds like the voice of a bird."

They said: " Come this way." I was surrounded by these beautiful friends and by clergymen — a good many clergymen there and they said some beautiful things — and they said: " Come to this window and see." But I said: " May I not hear them here? " I listened. In a moment the air was filled with the music of the different birds. Well, you have no conception of what that melody was like. I saw the birds. The birds were just as distinct, much more so than your own. The flowers are real, and as I go back to the mortal life and see the crudeness of it and see how I lived, the active energy and the active life that I then led, the energy which I put into that life, I wonder that I ever existed in it at all. Now you are not living in the real life. You are living in a dream, as it were. When you waken from the dream you will live, in the eternal life.

[At this point an acount is given of his asking to know something about Christ, to know whether he had been deceived in the earthly world in what he had been taught about Christ, and a description is given of a certain vision that was vouchsafed him. I have thought best to omit this whole passage, except to say that at its close he exclaims:]

And I live to tell you of it!

I walked about, I felt,— it was strange I had no hunger, no thirst, no desire to eat, no desire for food, but I am sustained by the conditions of the elements. The condition of the elements is such that we are fed and sustained and live by them. You can understand it perhaps vaguely if not clearly. You have a wonderful power to understand, or used to have. I think perhaps you can picture me and picture my home and picture my surroundings. At least, I make it as clear as I can for your understanding.

Now would you like to ask me any questions? Interrupt me if you wish to.

(Well, what do you do mostly with your time?)

Well, now I will tell you. What would correspond with your morning — we have no morning,— that is, it is all morning in a sense, in a way,— there is no daylight and darkness with us, it is all daylight — and what corresponds with your morning — I find that there are always entering into this life, there are spirits entering constantly from your life, and each one needs help, needs to be shown the way, and I enter the multitude, the throng outside of my own home; I pass through, I see the veil uplifted, I see a spirit passing in, perhaps millions of spirits. And I was told when I entered it that I must make this life here useful by helping others and by reverencing God, offering up gratitude in a prayerful spirit to Him who created me and gave me the privilege of this life here. And I do that through the so-called day, without fatigue, with perfect delight, assist some one spirit or more who have left the body and entered this life. And until they are fully conscious and realize where they are — some are taken from us, we are not allowed to see them at all, they are taken into another sphere; those are passed beyond us, we have nothing to do practically with them — but there are spirits that enter our own sphere, and we each lend a hand, show them their homes, settle them in it, go back and help another, and we are constantly doing that.

And then I feel sometimes that I would like to help in something that corresponds with your writing. I find in my home everything for which I ask. If I wish pencil, what corresponds with your pencil, I have it. If I wish to write my thoughts I can write them, if I wish to speak them I can do so, and every thought is granted, every desire is granted. And if I wish to lecture, as I often do, I can do so without fatigue, and it is helpful to those who enter this life. If I wish to write I can write, if I wish to walk I can walk, if I wish to sing I can sing, if I wish to speak I can speak. That makes the life, as you would understand it, perfect. It is a perfect life. And in order to live this perfect life you have got to live in that imperfect life, and the more you undertake to prepare for this life the less you have to go through when you pass it and the clearer your thoughts become when you enter it. Have you got the idea? Would you like to ask me anything? There are instruments all about me, everything you can think of — harps, violins, bugles, trumpets, horns, pianos, spinnet — do you remember what a spinnet is? All those instruments.

(They are just the same as our instruments, only better?)

Only better. Everything is beautiful, and it is in a way, each article, object, as well as spirit, is luminiferous. If the eye was opened to the spiritual and you could see me as I stand here talking with you, you could see every gesture I make, which is copied by Rector. He imitates me as I speak with you. You could see me and see my home, you could see everything that I have in it.

(Then what do you do in the afternoon?)

Then in the afternoon sometimes I write a lecture, I go out and look at my flowers, enjoy them; I go and visit others, they visit me. I learn to play on the instruments, the different instruments. I am absorbed in music and I love the flowers and the birds.

Then I feel as though I would like to take up some intellectual pursuit, and then I begin, and I am studying with those who have been here longer than myself the actual conditions of this life and what go to make up the life here, and as I learn I give it out to others, interpret my knowledge to others. Therefore our intellectual capacity is unlimited in a sense, and constantly being educated. And it is a beautiful idea, is it not? And then all through what you would call evening, during the evening, what would correspond with your evening, there is chiefly music going on, entertainment and music. Then after that passes, what corresponds with your early morning or late in the night, there are lectures and concerts of all kinds and descriptions going on, so that our lives are completely filled. And then during the later hours of the morning, before what would be your daylight, every single spirit on my side of the spirit life where I am [is] bowed in prayer for what would be at least two or three hours corresponding with your time, perfect devotion and a prayer.

(Then you don't have to sleep the way we do?)

Have no sleep, no rest. What corresponds with your rest is activity on our part. And then after the devotional exercises we are ready for what would correspond with your day for our work again. Can you conceive of anything more beautiful or more perfect, or more to the liking of a man with my tastes and my ideas?

(No.)

But man should live his allotted time in the earthly world to prepare to live and to live in this world, but if he takes his life intentionally or otherwise he remains in a sense like a little child here, or a germ, and he has to develop, unfold, bud and flower, and he must necessarily do so. Ask me anything you wish. I am so glad to tell you this because I want you to get some conception of what I am and what I am doing. This is not an idle, useless life here,— ah, no, not at all.

(How long does it take for you to come to me?)

[I meant at any time when I might think of him or call him, but I evidently did not make my meaning clear.]

I would seem some distance from you if you could see me as I am. When you have a desire to speak with me — there are spirits here who know *every mortal on the face of the earth;* that is, the same one does not know, but the different ones know every mortal — and they say: "Here is a friend, I think she is a friend of yours; there the Light is beginning to burn, it is open; we have attached the ethereal cord and we will remove the spirit from the Light, take it to our world or out on the cord, attach the cord to the shell, as it were, fill it with our ethereal light, and you can enter into it and see if it is your friend, and if so follow Rector, follow those that are used to the cord and go to the end of it and speak over it to Rector, who is actually within the shell himself, and he will transmit your messages to your friend." It takes in all, I suppose, of your time five or ten minutes perhaps for me to reach you.

[There is a brief talk about relationships, and I say:]

(You choose your own friends there, as here, don't you?)

Just the same.

. . . . .

It has been a perfect pleasure for me to see you again. Good-bye. God bless you. Come and see me again. May God watch over you.

Close

SITTING OF DECEMBER 20, 1904

[During the morning hours of the date given above, while my sitting was going on, another of Mrs. Piper's sitters underwent a surgical operation of some sort. I had not been told that an operation was to take place, nor do I know to-day who this person was. Rector explained to me that Imperator was obliged to be absent from the sitting, that he had left Prudens in charge while he, Imperator, was " over and around the cot " of a member of the circle. Near the close of the sitting, which lasted two hours, I was asked to take a message to Dr. Hodgson to the effect that the operation had gone on well. I noted the exact time when this was told me and sent the message to Dr. Hodgson by telegram at the earliest possible moment. I afterwards learned that the operation had gone on well, and that the person operated upon was much gratified on being told at an early hour what came from the Other Side of the Veil in regard to himself, communicated first to me, by me to Dr. Hodgson, and by the latter to the person concerned.]

Rector

[During the course of Rector's remarks I say:]

(Rector, wait a moment. Through whom is my friend going to talk now?)

He will try and speak direct to thee, if this be possible; if not I shall remain, as it were, a non-entity, giving his messages.

(You have allowed him to do that?)

Yes, I have, through the advice and command of our Leader.

. . . .

(Now, Rector, my friend is really and truly here almost exactly the same as if he were in his own body, is he not?)

Almost the same, and if thy spiritual eyes

could open thou wouldst see him standing here beside the ethereal cord, waiting his turn to enter into the Light upon the cord.

The General

Are you here?

(Yes.)

I am here to meet you. Oh how happy I am!

(Who is it? Don't be offended, will you?)

[Rattles off some lines of poetry, evidently some of the same words which came on the occasion of his first return, Dec. 23, 1903. I afterwards found the verse which he was quoting, which is by Charles Mackay, and runs as follows: —

Tell me, ye winged winds
  That round my pathway roar,
Do ye not know some spot
  Where mortals weep no more;
Some lone and pleasant dell,
  Some valley in the West,
Where free from toil and pain,
  The weary soul may rest?

This bursting out into some language which was rythmical, especially when he was happy, was most characteristic of him in life.]

Yes, the answer comes to me in the spirit, I have found it. I have found the rest, the life, the peace, hope, everything I hoped to find. . . . Now you know who it is?

(Oh, I know any way, only I thought I would just ask you that.)

Well, if you should say " General " I should be pleased to hear it.

. . . .

(When I first knew you I could not get used to calling you " General," but after I did get accustomed to it I could not call you anything else, because that seemed to be the right name for you.)

You thought it applicable?

(Yes.)

Well, that is pleasant. . . . Remember that the laws of vibration are very wonderful, very, very great, and my thought reaches you and *vice versa.* Therefore, for what more could I ask? [Something about his family doing well] My friends are loyal and I am happy, and the mere fact of my returning and speaking with you is an inspiration beyond description.

(Well, it helps me more than anything else I do.)

These good saints have helped me to understand the laws of communication, and I am not so much of an idiot that I should laugh at it or pooh-pooh at it further.

(Well, you would better not.)

How can I? The reality, it is a stern reality, and such a reality that it is the only thing which God hath given us to enable us to understand the laws of the eternal life. Is not that beautiful?

(Yes.)

Is it not beautiful? And it is the only way. So the casting off of the mere body, the shell, is nothing, it is nothing; it goes to waste, but my spirit lives to speak.

(General —)

Without the wires I could not communicate so easily, but with the wires my thoughts are registered clearly, are they not?

(Yes. General —)

Yes?

(You are taking Rector's place to-day, aren't you?)

For the first time I am, yes. Dear creature, he is here to help me, he stands beside me watching me to see that no harm comes to the instrument over which I speak.

(Well, it is not so very hard, is it?)

No, not hard, but if you were to question me one question after another it might confuse me, but you ask your questions so clearly, so slowly and in moderation, that I can understand them and reply. But if you were to fire questions at me, so to speak, volley after volley, it would confuse me so I should be obliged to go out. You understand?

(Yes.)

You look so well. . . . I see your spirit so clearly. I see what I did not use to see. I saw the physical and not so much the spirit. I see the spirit and the physical both combined. They both seem clear to me and beautiful. I am glad you followed out my instructions. I saw you in the place which I designated.

(Do you know where that is now? What do you mean?)

I saw you in a place with a lady, a very beautiful character, a very interesting character.

(Do you know who that is, or when it was?)

It is what we used to call summer, and it was in a green place, in a green place, and everything so beautiful, so peaceful.

[I spent several weeks during the preceding summer at a place called "Greenacre," in the town of Eliot, state of Maine. It is sometimes called "Greenacre-on-the-Piscataqua." Summer conferences have been held there for a number of years past, a large assembly-tent is erected on the greensward indicated by the name, and representatives of all religions are welcomed to the open platform.]

I saw you attending something seemed like lectures. I saw you conversing with an occasional gentleman, and I saw you sitting — it looked like a tent —

(Yes.)

— and saw you walking about.

(Yes.)

I saw you,— was it in a hammock? Something swinging.

(Yes, once or twice.)

And I saw you sitting there thinking, as it were, alone, and it seemed as though the shadows of night had fallen, and it was in the evening.

(Oh, yes.)

[I think it was at this point that I recalled a special evening. See explanation later.]

And I came and stood beside you and put my hand on your shoulder, and I heard you say, "how peaceful, how perfectly delightful it is." Do you remember it?

(Yes.)

Do you remember seeing the moon? The heavens seemed dark and then the moon appeared. It was early in the evening. And then I saw you get up, somebody came and spoke to you and you got up, walked about a little and went inside a building.

(I was in this hammock, I think twice, but one night a long time, and I even fell asleep there.)

Yes, that was the time when I put my hand on your shoulder and had the beautiful messages of peace from your spirit.

(Well, I went to sleep, oh very easily and beautifully, and I woke up and thought how beautiful it was to sleep there under the stars —)

Yes, stars, that is what I mean.

(— and I even got locked out of the house.)

Yes, yes, I know there was some difficulty in your getting in. I know that. And then I remember the surprise which came over you when you [recovered].

(Yes, I was surprised.)

And I was with you all through that little sleep, talking with your spirit. Do you remember what a peaceful wave came through you?

(Yes.)

It was I who sent it, who brought it.

(When I sleep like that it seems as if I was off somewhere; I am perfectly unconscious of this world, and where am I then?)

The spirit, your spirit, goes out upon an ethereal cord, just the same as the spirit of the Light here departs. Now I see the spirit of a woman going out, and it is the same in sleep, and I talk with your spirit just the same as I am talking with you now. Sometimes I almost feel that you will remember it, but when the spirit becomes active and fully possessed of the body and mind, then it forgets.

(Yes. Do you mean that is so always in sleep, or only in those occasional sleeps?)

Under certain conditions, only. The sleep

might be disturbed if the spirit communicated with it always, but upon certain occasions and under certain conditions we are able to talk with the spirit very, very clearly. The spirit understands and answers —

(You mean the earthly spirit?)

Yes, just the same as you answer me when I speak with you now. Why, to know that I can follow you, to know that I can see you in certain places and under certain conditions — and do you remember the tent?

(Yes, yes!)

Well, I saw you under the tent and sat beside you several times, and there was another lady with you. Who was that lady? She was a beautiful spirit, a bright, beautiful looking woman, a very clear mind and beautiful spirit. Is her name Sarah?

(Wait a moment. You know I am taking this all down, don't you, General?)

I do not see what you are actually doing. I see your thoughts are busy, very busy.

(I want to preserve every word. And it is so delightful to think that I can write down in shorthand just what you say, just exactly as I used to do when you were here.)

Oh, yes, I remember, that is what you are doing. Well, I do not actually see the writing going on, or the motion of your hand, or the — paper, is it? But I see you, your general outline, and I see you, as it were, in the light. You look as though there was a light all about you.

(Well, now let's be slow.)

That is the reflection of the spirit about you.

(My spirit?)

Yes, your own spirit. There is a reflection, as it were, all about you. It is very clear and very beautiful to me.

(Do you mean Sarah Farmer?)

I should not wonder. That sounds something like the name I heard her called by. She was not actually with you, but I saw you with her and saw you talking with her, and she has a very large spirit, a very broad spirit, and a very large and beautiful mind. Was that not so?

(Miss Farmer is the person who started that place and who has charge of it and has gotten all the fine speakers there, etc., and she is considered a very advanced spirit. Do you think it was she?)

Yes, it was she whom I saw.

(You know she was not a special friend of mine, though I know her.)

But I saw another lady, but I saw another lady with you —

(Well, General, wait a minute, wait a minute. How did you know her name was Sarah?)

I heard several ladies in a large room one

— you would call it evening again — calling — one spoke to her very intimately and called her Sarah, and I was within — I was perhaps — let me see — where is your hand?

[The psychic takes my hand and holds it about a foot from my face.]

I was within that distance, the distance that your hand is from your face, from her, when the name was called, and we can hear, and we can see and understand names as they are spoken in the body if we are attracted to any one individually.

(I see.)

And oftentimes the names, if we are interested, register themselves upon our memories and we never forget them. But to go back to this evening. Then you got in, didn't you —

(Yes.)

— all right, but that was the time when I saw you very clearly.

(Yes.)

[All the incidents referred to in the preceding conversation about Greenacre are almost literally true, though I am aware that some of them are simply things which one would naturally do during a summer outing. The sleep in the hammock, however, was an unusual one, and I have rarely, if ever, had one just like it. The fact is that I dislike the motion of a swinging hammock and seldom lie in one. The evening in question was one of those still, balmy evenings when it seems a sin to sleep under other canopy than the starry blue. I do not remember the moon, think there was none, or not until very late. I found an empty hammock a few rods from the Inn and appropriated it. I remember thinking how delightful it was to lie there facing the stars, entirely free from contact with the earth, a part of the atmosphere around me. I believe I even felt that I had been in error all my life thus far in not overcoming my dislike to the motion of a hammock. I fell easily into a sleep which must have been a deep one, and woke surprised to find from the general appearance of the Inn that it was late. I spoke with a gentleman who was passing, and as I remember I addressed him first. We went on the veranda, where there was one other person, and found that the Inn was closed for the night and we were locked out. Fortunately a parlor window was easily opened and then the door unlocked from the inside. I do not remember that I did, and think I did not, dream anything in the sleep which I could afterwards recall. I seldom heard Miss Farmer called Sarah, though that is her name. I was not specially with her, but probably spoke with her once or twice during my stay. I remember going to Greenacre one summer several years before the General passed away, returning and telling him about the place. That he ever heard Miss Farmer's Christian name spoken is very doubtful. He knew very little about her when living.]

(Now, General, why can't I learn to go out that way in sleep at will, almost?)

Well, it sometimes is not wise, sometimes it is not healthful, and it rests with the divine power as to when those conditions are suitable. Perhaps you can better understand that. I have learned a great deal about the conditions since I have been here, and it has been my one thought to study into the conditions and understand them for your sake, that I might be able to help you. I now see what a clear beautiful mind you had and why you were so interested in things which seemed to me rather absurd.

(Well, I am glad to hear you say that. All things come to him who waits.)

Yes, that is very true, but in the material life, in the mortal life, it seemed that I was unable with my peculiar make-up to grasp anything which I could not see.

(Yes.)

Therefore perhaps you will excuse me for not accepting your theories, but I lived to learn and understand for myself. It was a happy day when I came. The awakening was something beyond description. I never can tell you how I felt when I woke, and as my spirit passed up from that imprisoning body, through the cool ether, and the ethereal veil parted and my spirit passed through it into this beautiful world, the sensation and the light [delight] of it all is beyond my power to explain, and could I explain it in earthly words your mind could not really grasp it or understand it.

(Yes. General, you say that you could not accept things unless you could see them, but I thought you had a very fine and highly developed spirit, otherwise you would not have gone so quickly into the right conditions there and understood how to come back here, and be taken in by Imperator and Rector, etc., would you?)

You realized, I think, that my desire was for the advancement of mind, and you remember how I used to love poetry, and that I had a vein of sentiment, as you used to express it. Well, all that is fine spiritual perception; and it is really beautiful to me, now when I realize that I possessed that at all when in the physical body, and it has been a great benefactor to me in this life. You understand what I mean.

(Yes.)

It has been a great help, a great help to me, the mere fact of my growing in spirit in the body, and I really loved the beautiful.

(General, don't you remember how a beautiful woman used to impress you? Wait a moment — a friend of yours said once, old Mr. Clapp, that he did not know any man who took in the soul of a beautiful woman any more quickly than you did. We laughed over it, but I knew it was so.)

You understood it?

(Yes.)

Well, that is very beautiful, very kind in him to have said it. But I really think that I do, and know now that I did, I know that I understood women and the beautiful side as few men did in my environment or among my associates. And all those things appealed to me, and it was that that was highest and best. All that appealed to me most. And I was very happy in my earthly life in a way. I loved life for what life gave, and I loved the pleasures, and I loved the physical and all that the physical gave, but still I was large enough in heart, I feel, and in spirit not to allow the physical temptations to drown my soul.

(Yes.)

[This is a very good characterization of himself.]

. . . . . .

(I am of course very greatly blessed and privileged to have your continued friendship and to be allowed to come here and talk with you.)

Well, there are so many restrictions. This great spirit, this man here who leads, he is the noblest spirit I know, and there are so many restrictions,— he understands the conditions so well, and he has his everlasting eye open watching constantly that no harm shall befall anything or anybody connected or associated with the Light or the spiritual influences who work through it. Why, it is really marvelous.

(You mean Imperator?)

Yes. He is not present at the moment because he is away on a mission, but all those whom he does call, remember, really are privileged.

[See note at opening of this sitting.]

(Yes, indeed, they are. Now I want to ask you to watch, and if you think you are not going to have any more opportunities to come to me through this Light, then I want you to get one final chance if possible and tell me that you cannot come more. Will you try to do so?)

Will you repeat that once more for me? You mean that I must return here — and tell you before —

[Think I replied yes.]

Oh, yes,— well, I am going to tell you something. We call them the saints; they told me before I came here, before I asked them if I might speak with you, they told me that — the leader, the head spirit — he said that the conditions were low, but he said: "I will not go into explanation, but abide by what I say; the conditions are such that I must exert all my influence and power to hold the conditions in a sufficient state of clearness to enable you to return to your friends on the earthly side at all." Do you hear?

(Yes.)

And he also said: "By so doing, by doing this, you will be enabled to return through the Light occasionally for an unrestricted time —"

(Well, well, well, that is beautiful.)

—"and only under those conditions will you be permitted to return at all through the present Light." Therefore he has taken up the Light and is specially administering unto it to keep it for those who really need light and help. Do you understand?

(Yes.)

Well, if you do not perhaps Rector could make it clearer to you.

(I do.)

This was a private conversation between Imperator and myself, and he notified all the communicators who return through this Light of the conditions, and were it not for him and his wonderful power I perhaps should not be able to return, but so grateful are we to him that we offer up our blessings daily and almost hourly to him for his guidance and help. I wish you could see him.

[A few brief sentences only omitted here.]

I know one thing, I know that they all on our side can see and have predicted the absence of the Light on the other side of the water.

[It must be remembered that it was after the date of this sitting that Dr. Hodgson passed out. Mrs. Piper spent the winter of 1906–7 abroad.]

[In speaking of a prediction made concerning myself he says:]

Perhaps you had better ask Rector about that, as he is very clear and understands that very well; or, better still, George Pelham. Perhaps you know him? He has been a great help to me, a great help to me; although he is not so near the earth and the conditions surrounding the Light as I am at the present time, he really is a great help.

(Is he in another sphere, so called?)

Yes, he is in the last sphere, what you would speak of as heaven; the last, seventh sphere.

(What sphere are you in?)

I am in the third now. We have to pass through the third sphere in order to return, one might say, and therefore I could not return immediately directly I passed out of my body.

(Oh, that is the reason, is it?)

Yes. It is just like going from one room to another. [Illustrated by change of location in the material world] We advance until we feel that we have perfected ourselves according to God's will and idea, and then we are satisfied with ourselves, and not until we have.

(Well, when you first passed out did you go into the first sphere, or do you call this the first sphere where I am?)

Entering the material life is one sphere of life; that is the first, because life comes with the creation of the mortal body; life comes, it is the breath of God, and you are a branch of His great tree, you understand, and then the spirit grows, advances. Sometimes it does not advance in the mortal because it is hampered by physical ill, etc. If not, it is removed after a time and enters our life and then begins to develop and grow.

(Well then do you think every one leaves here just when it is right for him to go, whether he is young or old?)

Yes, yes, yes, that is all in the hands of God, and although we never see God — I have never seen Him and never hope to — He rules us all and reigns over us all, and we are a part, a branch of Him, and your question will make that clear to me.

(When any one dies, as we call it, whether he is thirty or eighty years old, it is the right time for him, do you think, or is death merely an accident, the time of death?)

Oh, it is not an accident. It is ordained by God. I could not understand when I was in the body why certain things [happened], why certain deaths took place, and so on, but God knows what their lives are and what they are to be should they live. Therefore He removes them perhaps through disaster, perhaps through accident, perhaps through fire, perhaps through loss of a vessel, and all that sort of thing, and He removes many at a time. But every spirit that enters this life, there is a home prepared for it and a place prepared for it. Perhaps you know that in the earthly Bible, the material Bible, "In my Father's house there are many mansions;" do you remember that?

(Yes.)

That has a literal meaning. . . . The spirit really never suffers, never knows a moment's pain or anguish of any kind. I know this from the — pure experience and study.

(But, General, you are not always, you over there, perfectly developed, and does not your happiness depend on your inner development there as it does here, your degree of happiness?)

Well, yes, to an extent, but we never suffer as suffering is expressed and understood by you.

(Yes, I see, I see. How about age there? How old are you compared with Imperator? What is the standard of measurement?)

Well, Imperator is — in fact, no spirit is ever old, there is no such thing as age with us. We enter this life according to our acts in the mortal life. If we have advanced and grown we have gained so much when entering this life, but if we are hampered by physical ills or physical infirmities, or perhaps some may inherit imbecility or something of that kind, when the spirit leaves the body it enters this life and grows, in a sense, as a child. It rests, it is released. The moment it is released from its body it assumes a condition of happiness, as it were. There is a peacefulness about it that permeates the whole spirit, and a certain power of understanding, and then it advances and grows until we are — we might put the age, for your understanding, to fifty, and we are never older than that in spirit.

(You mean never older than about what we think of as fifty?)

Yes. The body grows old simply but the spirit never grows old. The spirit remains young and beautiful always. No matter whether the man has passed from the earthly life through senile decay or through accident in youth, that makes no difference; the spirit is young always. But the conditions of the spirit and its happiness does [do] depend somewhat upon his advancement and growth and understanding and desires of right and wrong in the physical life.

(Well, supposing I have a friend now who goes over there, who did not think much of spiritual development here, could he be where he could see and talk with you, for instance, or would he be in a lower plane?)

Well, he would be — for your understanding — he would be in a somewhat lower plane upon entering this life, but if he has a great desire to reach me there are certain conditions through which he must pass in order for that desire to be accomplished, and if he lives according to the restriction and the laws which are mapped out for him here, then he might be able to see me in what you might term a few days. Then his desire would be fulfilled and he would be made happier in consequence.

(Now, General —)

Yes, I hear every word you say, and you have the faculty of speaking slowly and distinctly.

(Yes. When you went away, before your body was put in the earth, I was called by the Light known as Mrs. S. I went there after your body was put away, but she told me — that is, her control, her spirit guide told me — that the day you died — you passed out in the morning of our day here, and she said that you might have been around that day but she was so busy she did not notice you, but at night you were there and you had on such an anxious face that she had to listen to you, and you kept saying, "Send for Anne, send for Anne." Then when I went a few days later and talked with her she talked as if you were really there. Well, she said of course you did not put it in words, but she expressed the feeling. Now do you know anything at all about that, or were you around, or could you have been around, or could you have called me in that way? This is a Light to whom you went once with me when in the physical body.)

[The psychic known as Mrs. S. sent for me as explained above, asking if I would like a sitting, feeling that she ought to comply with the request of her control, though she had never before offered me a sitting simply because her control desired it, and never has since. Although she had seen in the papers an announcement of the death of my friend, she assured me that up to that time she did not know that I had been associated with him in business, having the impression that my special work was to assist Dr. Hodgson. On the occasion when the General accompanied me to a sitting with her, several years before his death, she was not told who he was and was not acquainted with him.]

Well, I remember after leaving my body, the first thing I thought of after leaving the body, after passing through this ether which I described and beyond the veil — that is, on our side of the veil, into this world — the first thing I thought of was, "Where is Anne? I will go and find her." I turned immediately and looked back into the physical world, into the material world, looked at the physical body, saw it like so much earth, and I saw you terribly distressed, as it seemed to me, and your spirit seemed very downcast and depressed, and I tried to reach you and was very anxious to do so and very anxious to make myself understood by you, and if she saw me she was probably true in saying it, because that was the first thing I remember of doing; and the first thought that crossed my mind was, "I will go and find Anne wherever she may be and tell her that I am still living and going on into the eternal life." Therefore I cannot contradict or disclaim her veracity.

[It was not his habit to call me "Anne" when living, though it is the habit of returning spirits to call their friends by their Christian names.]

(Now will you come to me as well as you

can whenever I go to see her, and do you think it would be well for me to go there occasionally?)

Yes, once in a while, but I have learned from Imperator, who knows all there is to know and prepares his messengers to give such light as he deems that they are fitted to give,— he says too frequent communication on our side is not wise, and it is wiser for the spirit to store up its knowledge and learn all the conditions of its life and then return occasionally, imparting that knowledge to his friend on the earthly side occasionally, but not too frequently, as the spirit loses by too frequent communication.

(I see.)

And it is not well for his best development.

[I tell him something about his old home.]

(I am going out there the evening preceding the fourth Sabbath from now, if I can. I am going to listen to the sound of your voice through the phonograph —)

A speech?

(Yes. Do you remember the phonograph?)

Yes, I do.

(There were some of your talks preserved. There was the remarks of Colonel Ingersoll at the burial of his brother, there was George Eliot's "Choir Invisible," there was Bryant's

"Flood of Years." Now I am going to listen to that for the first time since you went away, and I want you to stand right beside me all the time, and then when I come here again you can tell me about it.)

I shall be delighted. That will give me greater happiness than anything you could ask me.

[Unfortunately the phonograph was out of order when I made my visit.]

(Can you stay a while longer?)

Yes, I am listening.

[There is a little talk here about a sister in the body.]

You have a sister here in this world whom I have met.

(What is her name, do you know?)

No,— Hiram knows; at the moment I could not tell you, but he knows, and perhaps Rector will tell you what her name is. I remember I was introduced to her some time ago, and she is a beautiful spirit.

[This refers to an older sister, named Laura, who died in 1881, thirteen years before I became acquainted with my communicator.]

Then I have met your father. He was a peculiar man, wasn't he?

[Brief talk about my own family]

I like your father. He is a very strong

individuality, and he made his mistakes like other men in the earthly world, but he is a true spirit and he loves you all dearly.

[My father was "peculiar," a "strong individuality," and "made mistakes." He passed out four years before I knew my communicator.]

(Was your mother your guiding spirit all through your life here?)

Yes, and a dear one she was.

(Did you recognize her as soon as you saw her?)

She helped me, she showed me the way, she stood at my chair, the chair I used to sit in, she stood beside me when I passed out.

(Does she know me?)

Yes, you may rest assured that if I have had anything to do about it she does know you.

. . . . . .

[In speaking of my private work, I say:]

(You must not get discouraged if I get discouraged, will you?)

Not at all. That is not like me, is it? Didn't I have courage to the last? Ask me all you wish. My thoughts keep clear, as you ask your questions so clearly and beautifully that they are not confusing to me. If you were to say, "Now, General, I want you to find a name for me, get it now if you can,"

— in searching for that name, or switching my thoughts from the track on which they are flowing at the present time, over which they are flowing, it would confuse me so that I should lose the whole thread of my individuality and thought.

. . . .

The moment I entered this life I was told by Imperator: "You have just opened your life and your life is in the beginning. You have much to do with a friend whom you have in a sense left behind." . . . Then it dawned upon me what he meant. I said: "I know what you mean; you refer to the actual truth of a vague idea; it is going to be a reality,"— an idea which crossed my mind before my illness. It passed through my mind, the thought, before my illness, as I loved poetry, reading books, like yourself, everything,— it crossed my mind many times, and the desire that I might be qualified to write. When I entered this life Imperator pointed those things out to me. He made it clear to me that it was possible for me to return and help you and that we might do this thing together.

Now of course I cannot say how long the Light will remain in the body, or what the conditions are surrounding the Light, but I do know this, that conjointly and together on earth they have prayed and are praying and giving peace and restriction to the Light for a few who are privileged to use it and receive messages through it. Therefore I am one who is privileged, for which I am most grateful.

(Of course I do not want this wholly for my selfish pleasure. I want it to be of some use to the world, my coming here to see you.)

It should be, and if others would think likewise there would not be such a vague mystery about it all, as I used to think when I was in the body; there was a vague sort of unknowable mystery.

(The time is passing. I must not keep you too long.)

I must not remain too long, but Rector stands here ready to take me away, to assist me out, that no harm may befall the instrument through which I work.

. . . .

Tell me about little Augustus.

(Augustus? Which one?)

I mean the little fellow, the one they called — it is not really his name.

(Oh he is all right, very pretty.)

. . . .

But they call me now and I must go. I must not abuse my privileges. God bless you and be with you.

(Good-bye.)
You know I am Martin?
(Oh, yes!)

Close

SITTING OF MARCH 13, 1905

[There is very little that can be quoted from this sitting. It is a mixture of advice, prophecy, encouragement and reproof, on the part of both Rector and my communicator, relating to the carrying on of my work and to my condition of mind generally. Some of the remarks of my communicator are, however, so characteristically vigorous that I cannot refrain from giving a few of them as disconnected extracts.]

The General

Well, well, well! Will wonders ever cease! Is that you?

(Why, yes, don't you know me?)

Well, I guess I do.

(Is this you, General?)

Yes, that is right.

. . . .

I seem sometimes to see your fits of discouragement.

(Yes.)

I do not like it. I passed through life, I think, with a brave and a stout heart. Many disappointments and trials came to my life, but I never relinquished my hold, the hold upon my faith and trust and hope, all through my life, did I?

(No, I think not.)

[He *had* a faith of some kind, which carried him through to the very end without complaint.]

. . . . . .

Now I called upon these helpers and these holy fathers to bring you here that we might clear up some of these little cobwebs in your brain.

(Well, clear them up, I wish you would.)

. . . . . .

I dislike the sort of discontented thoughts. I dislike the feeling that there is no time, and a waste of energy, a waste of life, a waste of material, a waste of everything. Now that is not true at all.

. . . . . .

I thought you were an idiot, in a sense, because you believed in the eternal life, but how dense my mind was, how weak, how uncharitable! But you will forgive me, you do forgive me?

(Yes.)

You understand, but it was you that were wise and I was weak, yet I was your friend.

(I know that, General.)

I am your friend to-day. I look the same, and if your spiritual eyes could be opened you would see me standing here registering my thoughts through the ether with which this receptacle is filled.

. . . .

I can't have any thoughts of discouragement. Life is too serious, it is too beautiful, too strong, too great a thing to allow the thoughts of discouragement to enter such a brain as yours. I am astonished! I am astonished! "Oh," I said, "if I only get hold of her again I shall picture life as it really is and not as she thinks." What do you suppose you were created for? What do you suppose you were put into the earthly life for? You have not half carried out your mission. It is only in the beginning, and it is a useless waste of thought for you to think otherwise. Are you going to profit by what I am telling you?

(Yes, indeed.)

. . . .

I don't know whether I was a good preacher or not, but however, I know one thing, you usually profited by my advice, and I think you will do it now. In any case I shall watch you and I shall reach you now by sending you a message and you will know how things are turning.

[In omitted portion he speaks of his intention of sending a message occasionally "through that gentleman that comes here," meaning, of course, Dr. Hodgson.]

Why, the idea of a . . . physically well woman of your years and experience getting into such a state of mind! Why, it is dreadful, and if there was no charity in the world there would be no love, and if there was no love there would be no life, do you know that? And without — do you remember somewhere in the book we used to call the Bible it says unless ye have charity?

(Yes.)

Can you quote it?

("Unless ye have charity ye shall be as sounding brass and tinkling cymbals," I think.)

Yes, now register that in your mind.

. . . . . .

(Do you suppose you will be able to come here again this season?)

Oh, yes, I think so. The time, I don't know about that. You will have to ask them, and they will give you some definite idea. That is not in my hands. I only know that when the Light is burning and I see the Light, and the ether from our world is sufficiently clear, I know I can enter it and speak with you, which is a perfect delight. That makes our life on this side complete and perfect. You understand that. Now I want you to talk to me, but I did feel, oh if I could only reach you once more.

(Yes. Wait a minute. You know that the time has got to be short this morning, don't you?)

Short? What do you mean?

(Why, we can only have about half the time that we usually have, because the Light has not been in a good condition in the physical, and — is Rector there by you?)

Yes, what shall I say to him? You can see that the hands are always going out to us in touch. We are never left alone, I am never left alone when I am speaking with you. Imperator comes and goes, keeps coming and going, to see that all is going on well, and Rector or Prudens, some of them stand here and watch me to see how I get along, and if I fail for words or light they supply it. It comes over a line. Say what you want to. I think it is a pity to have you distressed about the time, but I don't know about these conditions so much, about the earthly side, but you will have to ask them, I think.

(Well, now I have been ordered to tell Rector that three-quarters of the time has gone and he will have only sixteen minutes more and then I shall have to leave, and if I do not I will not be allowed to come again. Do you understand that?)

You mean to say that I must go now?

(No, but I want you to tell Rector, who is there, just what I have said, will you?)

I will speak to him — just one minute.

[Very brief pause. Evidently speaking to Rector. Lips moving slightly.]

Well, what do you think he says?

(I don't know.)

Why, he says he does not see how he *can* open and close the Light in so short a time as that.

[I explain a little further the necessity for being brief, and there is a little more talk.]

(Well now, General, I am afraid you will have to go.)

[Still more talk]

(Now you will have to go, you will have to go,— good-bye.)

Don't say good-bye to me! I am going out and I will stand aside right here.

[Rector returns for a few moments.]

Close

SITTING OF APRIL 19, 1905

[This sitting was largely taken up with matters pertaining to my own family, one member of my family being very ill at the time. I had clear communications from my father and from my sister Laura, mentioned in sitting of Dec. 20, 1904. It seemed to me that Laura, for the first and only time, spoke directly through the machine, so called,— that is, spoke directly to Rector, who repeated her words. For she seemed surprised at the ease with which communication could be carried on, and said: "I want to tell you how clear I am, and what a perfectly clear line I am working over. I can see so much better than I ever did before." Upon this Rector immediately interjected the following remark: "I am going to say this, that I have never, I think, seen the Light clearer than it is this day." When I addressed my sister saying: "Now, Laura," she interrupted with: "I hear your voice like a trumpet." When I asked her to take a message to my father, she said: "I don't know,—if I could turn round and go out just a little distance on this cord I could bring him here. I will go and see." And then my father himself seemed to speak a few words directly. Other communicators were somewhat crowded out by relatives on this occasion.]

The General

[In speaking about my coming summer vacation, I say:]

(How about *Poland Spring?*)

Oh! [apparently laughing] Well, could you go there?

(I could go there for a short time. I think I will try and arrange to go to Greenacre a short time and then go to your old stamping ground, Poland Spring, where the water is, and the woods.)

And the Poland Spring House, you remember?

(Yes.)

Oh, I know so well. These old haunts last in my memory even in the spiritual world. The only thing I regret is the absolute imbecility on my part of the truth of an eternal life, but sometimes we have not the keenest spiritual perception into the higher things while in the mortal body, especially when the mind is troubled and disturbed with all that the earthly world places before us, and while life [lasts] we have not the time, perhaps, or the keen appreciation, and I may say apprehension, of the possibilities of the future. Therefore I made my mistakes in that line,— not exactly mistakes, but I lost a great deal.

(Yes.)

But my life was a busy one, as you know. Tell me about — how is little Gus, and Everett, and the children and all? They are doing splendidly, aren't they?

(Well, I think they are.)

. . . . . .

(Do you think I will not be able to come again this season?)

Well, I am not so sure. They said: "Now if you want to talk with your friend again we shall give you the privilege of doing it and the opportunity will present itself immediately," and then they said: "We will appoint the third day," and so on, and then they made it known to somebody in the body, and they said: "Because we cannot at the moment see the probability of it again." But if it is possible and you are called for, you know you have got to come.

(I gave up a good deal this time to come.)

Yes, I know, but it could not be avoided, and it was better so, as you can see. And haven't you found them very clear to-day?

(Yes, very.)

And I myself, the only thing I regret is that I have to cease to speak. . . . Now I am going. I am not going to say good-bye, because I hate the word.

Close

SITTING OF JUNE 21, 1905

. . . . . .

What is life is love, and what is love is life, and what is life and love is spirit. I have called you here again. I have felt that I could not allow the Light to close without meeting you once more. . . . . You have freed me, did you know it? Nothing on the earthly side hampers or troubles me in the least. I am as free as it is possible for a spirit to be.

. . . . . .

Your father sends a great deal of love to you, and also your sister. She is so much freer since the last conversation with you here that she is the happiest girl you ever saw. You have helped them greatly by coming here. You have no idea of the relief to the spirit these communications give.

(Give my love to them both.)

. . . . . .

I understand that they are going to make better conditions after they return.

["They" means the spirits in charge. "After they return" means after the vacation season.]

I understand that Imperator has made special arrangements — do you know what they call an hour?

(Yes.)

They are going to prolong it an hour and a quarter at the very least, and they are going to make the earthly friend sign to their arrangements —

["Earthly friend" is the expression which was commonly used by the trance personalities in referring specifically to Dr. Hodgson.]

— because right in the middle of conversation, sometimes when the best sentiments are to be given, the Light is shut off, and this is not quite right. I lose the counts of time, only that the man who has charge —

(Hodgson?)

— Hodgson, he keeps talking about hours and fifteen minutes, hours and three-quarters, and so on, and that keeps it fresh in the memories of the controls.

. . . . . .

(Tell Rector that there are fifteen minutes — the rule.)

Who says that?

(Hodgson says that.)

[Meaning that I had been directed to bring the sitting to a close at a certain time.]

Does he? Well, he is a good fellow. He receives much help. I will tell you a secret — he is inclined to be jealous, a little bit hostile if he cannot have his way, but they manage him over here beautifully. He knows that whatever they say is right and he must obey, if we return. Do you know that I feel sometimes it is possible that we may not get at this Light, and then what shall we do? Imperator has been trying to make rules and regulations that when the Light is dim and unsatisfactory he will only see those who really deserve and let the testing go, fearing that the

Light may give way entirely. But at the present time through his prayers he has kept it very well and done well. Does not that in itself show the power of spirit?

. . . . . .

Close

SITTING OF DECEMBER 20, 1905

The General

Well, are you really here again? I see, I hear, I understand. Your spirit looks clearer to me. Are you not happier?

(This is the General, is it not?)

Yes, and no one else.

. . . . . .

(I want you to understand, and Rector and all of them, that I fully and most thoroughly appreciate the privilege of coming here to see you.)

Divine Providence governeth all things well, and as I must say, in harmony with these good friends here, that if you have faith and trust, all things are mapped out for good and will be seen by yourself as being managed by the Unseen, in the main.

(Yes.)

You understand?

(Yes.)

And what is God's will, will be done.

Therefore your coming here is a privilege to us as well as to yourself, and it is in obedience to His will.

[" Obedience," stumblingly, first, then " obeyance " or "abeyance "]

(Yes.)

How can we manage it otherwise? What can we do when you are summoned?

(You may be sure I shall be on hand.)

And the way will be opened for you. Let me speak on, because we are limited on our Light. That is, the power gives out. . . . I am very anxious, since I have learned so much about this beautiful life and realize the truth and reality of it by having the actual experience, that the world should through your hand and brain be made cognizant in part of the unfoldment, of the true development of the soul after it leaves its environment; that it is an active consciousness, that it is in the state of higher development, that it is able to reach the physical plane and act through such voices as your own, we would say, to give expression and utterance to the truth and reality of in part what this life contains. Is that clear to you?

(Yes. Well, of course I cannot know about your life except as you give it to me.)

But through your own unfoldment, as you say, you receive constantly help and impressions from me in this life.

(Yes.)

You cannot work alone without this help which you receive perhaps unconsciously to yourself, yet not unconsciously to — your subconscious mind receives the impressions which I give you and they are unfolded through the conscious mind. Therefore you give expression to the very things which I impress your mind with.

. . . . . .

Tell me about the boy.

(Well, what do you see about him?)

[I have in mind a nephew of mine, who lives in California, in regard to whom I have had many communications, but his reply indicates that he is inquiring about his own boy, and I say:]

(Do you mean my boy or yours?)

I mean mine. . . . In regard to your boy, he is a long distance in the earthly world, is he not?

[This thought was evidently suggested by something which was said about his own boy being nearer to me.]

And is that not his child?

(What child?)

Has he not a child or two?

(He has one, or has had one.)

Is this not his?

(Where is it?)

Why, isn't it here? Isn't this Max's boy? His name is Plumb.

[My nephew's name]

(Well, that is his child, yes.)

Well, I wanted to tell you about him, because he came up to me, and as I found him I said, "Why, this child certainly belongs to my friend in the body," because he was so constantly — do you remember a spirit named Laura?

(Yes, my sister.)

Yes, with her.

(Well, *is* it my sister, or some one else named Laura?)

Yes, it is another, it is somebody else, but I told you about her, did I not?

(I think it must be some relation. I wish you could see.)

Well, they are both here, the lady and the child. And the child leaving the body was a great disappointment to him, but it was better for the child and infinitely better for him and for the mother.

(Why?)

Because the developments would have been very painful. God knows best, and to unfold His truths would take me a long time.

(Well, we won't try now. Is that my grandmother who has the baby?)

Yes, it is your sister's grandmother — that

would be yours, of course, certainly — well, you know we look at the connections here. She is an elderly lady, an elderly lady, but in the spirit no one is elderly. Perhaps you can understand contradictory statements, if possible. Her name was Laura.

(Yes, that is it.)

She is very much attached to that child.

(Well, I have heard through another Light that this grandmother of mine had this child. Now have you seen me with that Light lately at all?)

Yes, yes —[quite eagerly]— what Light was that? I have been trying to give you a password.

(At that time?)

Yes. You did not seem to understand it some way.

[This child; a babe of nine months whom I had never seen, died Sept. 25, 1905, three months previous to date of this sitting, no sitting with Mrs. Piper having taken place in the interim, and this is the first reference by her to it. On Dec. 8 of this same month, less than two weeks previous to date of this sitting, I had a sitting with the psychic known as Mrs. S., who told me that this child was with my grandmother, and that my grandmother and my communicator were acquaintances and friends. I took it to be my mother's mother, as my father's mother died when I was a mere child. My mother's mother I knew well, as she did not pass away until I had grown to be a young woman. She was a reader of books on Spiritism and was much interested in the subject, though she had few sympathizers among her own friends. She is the grandmother who would be most likely to have the child, and her name was Laura.

It will be seen that when my communicator asks: "Do you remember a spirit named Laura," I immediately reply: "Yes, my sister," the sister being the first thought in my mind. This positive reply might well have switched my communicator's ideas off the right track, but when I say: "Is it my sister, or some one else named Laura," he replies: "Yes, it is another, it is somebody else, but I told you about her, did I not?" I do not know to what this "I told you about her" can possibly refer, unless it means that my communicator was actually present at my sitting with Mrs. S. two weeks before, and that he was the one who impressed it upon the psychic to assure me that the child was with my grandmother.]

But I wanted to tell you that this little child is very happy and is in a home of its own with these people and that they are taking good care of it, and that there is nothing lost.

(You tell both those Lauras that I am much pleased to know that the child is with them and will so report to the parents.)

That is right.

. . . . . .

Why, spirit, spirit travels, remains conscious, feels out to its friends, reaches them on the earthly side, but there are some things which its memory cannot and does not wish to retain. There are pages in every book of life which the spirit when it leaves closes that book in the mortal life, it would like to forget, and so it does. Therefore it is happier.

(General, are you in a sort of zone around the atmosphere of this earth, and can you go to other planets and stars if you wish?)

Yes, certainly, and now there is a case here which has been very peculiar and perhaps has been commented upon in the mortal body — doubtless it has, because I have seen this man struggling here and then I have seen him depart suddenly. He would come to the Light and the Light would not be open, and he would take his departure and go way off to another country. His name is Myers, or Myer.

[I think my communicator in life knew nothing about F. W. H. Myers, of England, who died in 1901, the year preceding that in which my communicator died.]

And he comes here, he finds the Light unopen — a very active, brilliant, fine man, keen perceptions, finest type of mind — and he comes here, he finds the Light not burning, he departs, he goes and looks after his family — he has a family in the mortal body — he goes to find them and remains with them, and oftentimes when the Light is burning he fails to appear, but you can understand that because of his absence from the Light and being among those he loves.

(Well, does he go to other worlds?)

He goes to other worlds and other planets. He is constantly studying — he is a great student — he is studying the conditions and the changes and the whys and the wherefores of communication, and the laws of life in the spirit, in the body, and the ways of God and the ways of man and spirit in general.

(Now I am afraid you will have to go.)

Shall I have to go? —

(Tell Rector —)

— but with you I shall be —

(Tell Rector —)

— the way will be open when I can return again soon and finish my conversation, for I have much to tell you which I cannot utter to-day.

Close

Note. This sitting took place on the morning of the day on which Richard Hodgson died. His death occurred in the late afternoon or early evening.

SITTING OF APRIL 17, 1906

[This sitting took place in my own private room, near Copley square, Boston. The "earthly friend" means Dr. Hodgson.]

The General

Hello, hello, hello! Well, well, well! What have you got to say to me?

(Who is this?)

Well, well, well! Hello, Anne! Where did you come from? Where did you come from? I should like to know where we are, where you are, where we all are, where I am. Well, well, well! I am the General. Oh, dear! Oh, dear! And you did not know me, did you? Well, I never thought the time would come when you would not know me.

(Well, wait a minute, General.)

What are you doing, writing?

(Yes.)

Oh, I see. Well, well, well you were always writing. Were you ever doing anything else?

(Now, General —)

Yes, yes!

> Tell me not in mournful numbers,
> Life is but an empty dream,

And the soul is dead that slumbers,
And things are not what they seem.
Life is real, life is earnest,
And the grave is not its goal;
Not enjoyment and not sorrow,
Was not — no —
Dust thou art, to dust returnest,
Was not spoken of the soul.

(You have not forgotten your poetry, have you?)

No, and I never shall.

(General —)

Yes?

It matters not how straight the gate,
How charged with punishments the scroll;
I am master of my fate,
I am captain of my soul.

That is not original, but I love it.

(Now, General, do you know you spoke so much like the earthly friend when you first came —)

Well, he was right beside me, and he was so determined that he would speak first, I was trying to see if I could not get him to give his consent to let me, without him, and he first entered and then he stepped aside and let me enter, and that was how that happened to be.

(Then that is the reason I did not quite recognize you at first.)

Well, I forgave you long ago. I don't lay

that up against you. I know it is difficult because you cannot see me. You see, being a spirit, I am so fine, my ethereal body is fine and so finely constructed and all, that you cannot see it with your mortal eye, but with your spiritual eye you could see me plainly. Are the children all well? Are you well? Busy? Busy as a bee.

(Well, wait a moment, General. I am sorry I cannot talk faster —)

Talk and write too? Well, the body has its limitations, you know.

(Yes, I guess that is so. Now you said, " where are we all." Now I want to know if you know where you are, actually are, in this spot this moment.)

At the present moment?

(Yes.)

Well, may I look around a bit and see?

(Yes.)

Well, now just give me time.

[Fingers of hand touch my face, rest a moment over my own hand, then find cabinet size photograph of my communicator in gilt frame which stands on table within easy reach. This occupies only a minute or two. Then emphatically:]

Ha! ha. You can't fool me! I am in your room! That is *myself*, that is *myself!*

(Yes.)

I am in your room. Well, I am more

pleased than I can say. This is an unexpected pleasure and a perfect delight to me. Well, I must say I am happier for it. How does it happen? Perhaps you need not take the time to explain, perhaps somebody else will do it for me, but I am just a little bit in a quandary to know how it happened. Oh, what a fool I was! I did not know, I did not realize that I should live again, and of all things I least expected to return.

(The daughters of the Light were ill, and so the Light has remained away from them, and the meetings have been in this room of mine for some little time past.)

That is the reason why I was so attracted here that I begged Rector to arrange for me to speak to you.

(I see.)

I had all I could do to keep from interrupting each time lately.

(Yes.)

Well, that accounts for it. You see that helps me to understand. Thank you very much.

[This was the first private sitting of my own which took place after the passing out of Dr. Hodgson, although I had attended many sittings during the winter as assistant and recorder, and had been recognized by the Hodgson personality, for it must be understood that Dr. Hodgson purported to return through Mrs. Piper *very* soon after his death. That is a matter, however, which I am leaving for others to present. But his manner of salutation was something like what appears in the opening remarks of this sitting. In fact, the two personalities seem to be blended, probably indistinguishably so to the reader to whom both men were strangers when in life, though the peculiar characteristics of each are quite apparent to me. The profusion of exclamatory greetings is Hodgsonian, while the irrepressible bursting into rythm is Martinian.]

. . . . . .

Now haven't you got anything to say to me? I want you to say lots of things to me.

(You will let Hodgson come a few moments before —)

Oh, he is coming, you cannot get rid of him so easy. You know this is a great big telephone and I am speaking into it.

(Explain it more, will you?)

Yes, I will. The telephone is filled with ether from our world, and it is a receptacle, a vessel, and we blow into it just exactly as you would blow a bellows, the air through a bellows to an open fire, into an open fire, and then we attach a cord, an ethereal cord, to that and talk right over that cord right into the machine, and make this machine utter our thoughts.

(I see.)

. . . . . .

(Now, General,—)

Hodgson is coming!

(Tell him to wait a moment.)

Yes, good fellow,— I am glad to know him.

[Dr. Hodgson and my communicator were not acquainted during life, though each knew something about the other.]

. . . . . .

There is a lot more I wanted to say, but I am afraid I won't have the strength.

(Well, the time is very nearly up, and I suppose I must speak with Hodgson. At any rate, I want to.)

Well, he is going to, but I am going to see you again sometime. . . . I suppose I must step aside. . . . This is the most wonderful thing in the world to-day. . . . I must step aside and let this gentleman speak. Good-bye. It is *au revoir*, not good-bye.

(Good-bye, General.)

[" This gentleman " means Dr. Hodgson, with whom I hold a brief conversation, which I have thought best not to insert.]

Subliminal

[When Mrs. Piper is coming out of trance there are brief remarks and broken utterances, some of them very clear, some of them in a whisper, some of them quite indistinct and wholly unintelligible. The appearance is as if she were taking a last look at spirits standing near, and as if these spirits, while she is returning to her body, were impressing upon her mind words and messages for her to repeat to the sitter. Some of her broken utterances also indicate her returning perception of her surroundings in the room where the sitting has taken place.]

Getting dark. They are all going away.

[Muttering something unintelligible]

I wonder what Martin has his hand in it — General Martin is — I don't know you —

[Looking up inquiringly]

I can't hear you —

[Making great effort to hear]

What? I am happier for it. She'll understand. It is all right with me. I hope it is with her.

[It will be noted that " I am happier for it " is the same phrase as that used by my communicator through the trance, as if he were repeating to Mrs. Piper's returning spirit some of the same language used to me while she was unconscious of what was being transmitted through her organism.]

Close

SITTING OF JUNE 6, 1906

[Permission had been given for my sister Grace, Mrs. Moore, to accompany me on this occasion. She was present at the opening of the sitting and at its close.]

The General

. . . . . .

(I have copies of all that you have said to me here, and I do not think it will all be published by the Society, so that leaves the coast clear for me to publish something in my book, and I propose to do that, and speak of your life in Boston.)

Very good. I should like that very much indeed, because I do not care now. I lived to know the truth, to understand the truth and to speak the truth, and the truth will live, and I am not ashamed of my name or anything associated or connected with it, and the truth will bear its weight throughout the universe, and I think it is better to be frank and open and honest with the name.

. . . . . .

I heard a little music in your room the other evening and I heard an instrument being played, and I sat in a large chair right near the table. You were apparently reclining.

(Was somebody else making the music?)

Yes, yes. It was your sister, I think.

And you were reclining, and I was sitting in the large chair and listening.

(That was lovely.)

And I heard it all. And then I heard —

(Do you want my sister to come in the room now?)

I am afraid it will interrupt me. I heard "Old Oaken Bucket" plainly.

(Was my sister playing that or was I?)

You were playing it.

(Well, that is one of my favorites.)

Well, I don't know it at all. I know I heard it. I heard you play it. I caught the air. Then I heard her play a religious thing, religious piece.

(Now, General, wait a moment. My sister is just outside. I think I will call her in, but you need not speak to her unless you wish.)

I am afraid it will interrupt me. I thought it might interrupt my thoughts.

(When I am alone in my room I sometimes sit down and play a little bit, and often play "The Old Oaken Bucket.")

Yes, yes, I hear that. Well, I heard that. Then I heard another little one that sounded like "The Suwanee River."

(I did not play it.)

No, your sister. She played a few bars of it. And then I heard a waltz, a waltz being played. I think she has a very pretty touch, and I think she sings a little, doesn't she?

(Oh, yes.)

But why doesn't she sing? I heard her humming but not much singing to it.

(Well, her throat troubles her a little now.)

She is not well, but the spirit will improve the flesh.

[I do not play much, and do not play often, but probably play the "Old Oaken Bucket" oftener than any other one piece. I did not play it on the evening referred to. This sitting took place on Wednesday. On the preceding Friday evening I was in my room with my sister, Mrs. Moore, who was then visiting me, though she had not been with me for nearly a year prior to this visit. A friend of hers called, and during the evening my sister, who is very musical, sat down at the piano. I betook myself to a couch, decidedly reclining. The friend sat in a small rocker, and the Morris chair, the largest chair in the room, which stood near the centre table, was unoccupied. My sister's playing is noted among her friends for its remarkably pretty touch, and she has a way of humming at times when she does not feel able to sing. As I remember this evening she sang in a low tone at first, and finally sang one or two songs in her natural manner. She tells me that she played just a few strains of the "Suwanee River" on the evening in question, though I did not remember it and could not have told that she did play it.]

. . . . . .

Close

SITTING OF SEPTEMBER 26, 1906

[There is on this occasion quite a long conversation with Dr. Hodgson. This and Rector's talk occupy the larger portion of the hour.]

The General

Here I am. I am delighted to see you. How are you?

(I am fine. Don't you think so?)

Good. Isn't that splendid! Yes, I think you are. I never saw you better. Did you ask your sister about that music?

(Yes.)

Well, wasn't I right?

(Yes, you were. She played the "Suwanee River" that night, but I did not know it.)

Yes, and you often play the "Old Oaken Bucket?"

(Yes.)

. . . . . .

Do you know that I am with you when your body is in repose and your spirit is floating around conversing with me? Do you remember it when you wake? What are you doing? Are you writing?

(General, I have to write down every word. I wish I did not.)

Why don't you split the difference and divide your mind?

(Well, I will. It hinders me. I think I will drop it now.)

I wish you would. You lose the personality.

[Which means that I discard paper and pen, sit close to Mrs. Piper, and have an easy, natural conversation with my communicator.]

Close

SITTING OF AUGUST 5, 1907

[The date of this sitting is a little out of season. Mrs. Piper had just returned from England and gave a few sittings before leaving Boston again to spend the remainder of the summer in the country.]

The General

Little rills make wider streamlets,
  Streamlets swell, the rivers grow;
And they join the ocean billows,
  Onward, onward, as they go.

Does that sound natural?

(Yes. Will you say that once more?)

[Verse repeated]

(All right, that is natural. How do you do, General?)

Well, how do *you* do? I do as I'm a mind to most of the time.

. . . . . .

Do you realize that even though I go on in life, progressing in this life, and go step by step, my spirit is improving, I still look back, and never a step forward do I go that I do not look back and live in pleasant memories always of the old, olden days. . . . I have enough sentiment in my nature which has become a part of myself and my spirit here that if I sound or seem sentimental you must overlook it, because it is a part of the spirit.

(You cannot be too sentimental for me.)

I know your nature, but I say that sentiment is a part, and a finer, higher part, of the spiritual life and its existence. And life is love and love is life, and life is love, therefore it is universal.

. . . . . .

[In speaking about the mediumistic power of another psychic, he concludes by saying:]

Well, ask Hodgson. He will tell you. He has been a great help to me over here, and he has been helping Myers all during the burning of the Light. Perhaps you don't know what has been going on?

(Not much.)

Well, perhaps it is just as well if you don't. I don't know very much about it myself, only I know we are very pleased on this side.

[This doubtless refers to the work of the season just closed. See Proc. S.P.R. Part LVII, Vol. XXII, October, 1908.]

[Toward the close of the hour my communicator says:]

But I am going to ask Hodgson what part of his reports he wants you to have and he will tell you.

(The time is up.)

I must let him come.

(The time is up.)

Well, he has got to speak to you, I can't help it. It is not good-bye, only *au revoir*.

[A brief talk with Dr. Hodgson follows, at the close of which he says: "God bless you, and stick to it. That is the advice of your old friend R. H."]

Close

SITTING OF NOVEMBER 20, 1907

[There is very little that can be quoted from this sitting. I held conversations with three communicators, and my old friend Hiram Hart sent a brief message of remembrance. More than twenty-four years have elapsed since he passed away. This is the occasion on which my communicator says that "delays are dangerous" and he now wishes me to push my work along as rapidly as possible. While advising and urging me, he says:]

The General

You are a little bit stubborn, do you know it? You get an idea and you want to carry that idea, you analyze it, you say it over in your mind, and you are inclined to go back to the first idea. Sometimes the broadest and most reasonable minds are willing to add an idea to their oldest idea, and have two ideas instead of one.

(Well, I hope I am.)

[Further on he says:]

Imperator calls you one of his children. I suppose you must be.

(I am glad to know that.)

Well, he watches over you with his all-seeing eye and does not want you to fail or fall into error.

. . . . . .

Close

SITTING OF JUNE 17, 1908

The General

. . . . . .

You have heard of pearly gates and streets of pearl? Those were as real as any expression which you may use in the physical life. More real. It is a fact,—there are streets of pearl, gates of pearl.

(Just like our pearl?)

It is similar. Yes, the comparison is so near that you could not mistake it for a moment. And our castles, our homes, are real. They are as real to us as yours are to you. Yours is simply the imitation, ours is the real. We have streets, we have gardens, we have homes, we have rivers, we have lakes. If we bathe in the river our garments are not wet, but still we are purified, we are cleansed. But the natural hair — but entering it does not saturate our garments, and it does not wet what you call the hair. We come out and it is light and dry, the garments are dry, but the soul is purified by bathing in the waters. Is that clear to you? We walk about the lakes, we walk in the gardens, we meet friends, we commune with friends, we hear music, we hear sermons, and we pass our time glorifying God and living in His presence, in a sense,— understanding what His hand hath created and what He has blessed us with, eternal life.

(When you go out of your mansion and look up toward what would be our sky, what do you see?)

We see above us, we see our world radiant, filled with light, a beautiful, soft moonlight, difficult for you to comprehend because it is so clear, so beautiful, so light. We do not see what you see — stars — but we see this beautiful moonlight above us, all round us. The air is scented with the most delicious perfume. It is so exquisitely delicate that it seems almost a part of our own existence, it is so beautiful, so delicate, and so real. And we see above us this beautiful light, and it is what you would call in your world the heavens. It is above us, far above us, and we see at times, we see — a face appears. It grows lighter at times, especially when we are in a particularly happy state. The face appears over us and we know it is the face of Christ. We hear the swishing of the garment, as it were, and then it passes off and some one else receives the vision.

(Do you ever see any other face like that in the heavens except that of Christ?)

We see what you would call — there are saints administering to those who need help, or perhaps have just passed over, have not understood the conditions, and these saints appear to give them courage and to give them faith and to show them that this is everlasting and eternal life. I am not very good at preaching.

(Then you do not have our beautiful firmament of stars at night?)

We have what corresponds to your stars. There are rays, as it were, little flickering rays all through the firmament, all through the heavens. We see these little rays all about us, this beautiful figure passing, we see another face and then another as it passes. Why do we not come into closer proximity with them, as we say? Because they are superior even to ourselves, they have progressed, they have gone on to a higher, even, sphere than our own. That is, they are the controlling, the ruling forces, and govern our own life and our own world. Do you understand?

(Yes.)

A word of command, simply a hand is raised — we know its meaning, we understand it, we sense it as a little child would sense danger, or a sensitive animal would sense danger.

. . . .

Subliminal

[I have not exact notes of what Mrs. Piper said on this occasion while coming out of trance, but I have a memorandum that she mentioned the names of nearly all my special friends on the Other Side, as if she were seeing them:— Hiram Hart, the General, my sister Laura, my father, the baby, my grandmother, Pickett. My grandmother holds the baby up and the baby sends love to its mother, and just then the General picked a rose and handed it to the baby, and the baby was picking it to pieces. The psychic, gradually returning to consciousness, calls this one of the most beautiful sights she ever saw.]

And the End is Not Yet. September, 1909.

PART III

SUGGESTIVE THOUGHTS ON THE ATTAINMENT OF SPIRITUALITY

As I have previously said, I have no System of Philosophy to present, and possibly nothing which ought to be dignified by the name of Philosophy at all. I have not, however, been able to divorce my psychical research from my religious feeling, nor do I see how any religion can be worthy of the name which does not enter as a continual inspiration into the daily life. Among the many definitions of religion which I have seen I like that best which makes it mean the right relation of mind and heart toward our fellow-creatures and our environment, and the right attitude of the soul toward the Incomprehensible and the Unknown. It need have no specific name, nor is it of great importance that one be identified with some particular religious sect, but it *does* devolve upon each individual person to ascertain to the best of his ability what attitudes and relations *are* right, and to constantly enlighten his understanding on these matters as he progresses along the pathway between birth and the grave. We love the man who walks in our midst with his head among the stars, but we smile a little at his lack of mental balance if he does not make sure that his feet are treading solid ground. I believe we may walk on solid ground and at the same time lift the eye to the most distant star whenever we may wish.

I have ventured to offer a few ideas upon the varied relationships in life. If they shall be found to be old, that will matter little, since every one is privileged to appropriate from out the treasure-house of the Past, to recast old ideas into new moulds of his own thinking, and to nourish himself thereby. It may be that many of my readers will choose to pass by these pages altogether, yet deep down in my heart I am assured that among those who peruse them there will be found at least a few other hearts in which they will awaken an answering thought and a responsive feeling.

SELF-DISCIPLINE

The best is near, already ours,
If we would wisely use the powers
    Of mind and heart
    And do our part.

Complete and fair the earth will be
For him whose inner majesty
    Crowns every sight
    With its own light.

In any place we find the thing
That in our hearts the power we bring
    To see and use,
    All else we lose.

—VICTOR E. SOUTHWORTH.

SELF-DISCIPLINE

TO EASILY ignore one's own personality is an attainment that must be striven for, a power that must be gained, but it is after all a mere preparation for that which follows, a mere opening at the door to the Vastness which is outside of personality.

DEATH of the lower means the birth of the higher. The suppression of a vice means the nourishment of a virtue. The dying of the selfish means the living of the charitable. The extinction of the ignoble means the blossoming of nobility.

SOUL culture certainly does not come from the reading of many books or from the forming of a large acquaintance, nor is it measured thereby. Yet it may depend somewhat upon the nourishment one is able to extract from his reading and upon the society of those of his acquaintance who themselves are cultured.

ONE who is extremely sensitive and at the same time self-repressed — the first condition generally being the cause of the second — is the possessor of a temperament sufficiently at war with itself to cause any amount of mental anguish until the temperament is understood and the unhappiness resulting from it is outgrown. Yet this same sensitiveness when once understood, when it serves and does not master, brings to its possessor the perception and enjoyment of untold things which the person lacking it or possessing it in small degree cannot appreciate at all. Slowly in early life we begin to apprehend the great truth that as surely as the cause of our unhappiness lies within ourselves just so surely do we possess the power within ourselves to remedy ills, to dispossess ourselves of misery and to take possession of bliss.

I UNDERSTAND the philosophy of Spinoza to make a distinction between necessity and external compulsion. We are of necessity, in the nature of things, bound to do certain actions, to follow certain lines of conduct. That is, we *need not,* unless we choose, but we *must* in order to attain our highest good. That is all.

THE giving up of the selfish quest for happiness so dignifies and ennobles the soul that one ceases to grope with downcast eyes; one looks up, takes the hand of God and walks with Him as a companion, a friend. Then there is work in plenty to do, for one is a co-worker with God. Just as a grown-up daughter takes the arm of her earthly father and walks joyously, confidingly, companionably, sharing his schemes and his outlook, yet recognizing all the while the superior age, the superior knowledge, the superior power.

THE person who is delicately sensitive to spiritual influences receives impressions in many ways and is more or less swayed by them, and it is particularly desirable, indeed imperative, that such person should cultivate strength and self-control.

MY own nature is my law. That law in its purest meaning *must* be obeyed.

LET us never forget, in the analysis of self, that the great desideratum is the power to turn one's face immediately and wholly in the opposite direction from that of our sensations, our emotions, our personal desires; to be and to do as if they were not; to fling from us the encumbrance of self-analysis itself, and to stand erect as free, pure spirit.

WHEN one accepts the theory that the haps and the mishaps in his particular environment take place for the purpose of developing character in *him*, to understand their significance and their special bearing upon the end in view becomes a fascinating intellectual game.

TO control one's nerves or be ruled by them — that is the question. The one thing leads to life, the other to death. "Self-stayed, serene and high," the poet says. It seems to be an inversion of the natural order of things that *mere nerves* should have possession of the field, frightening all else. Yet the nerves are like the finest magnetic needle, indicating the slightest change in the atmosphere, the least deviation in our course. They should be of the greatest aid to the spirit, like the dainty, delicate servitors that they are.

SELF-POISE is a marvelous thing. Its influence ramifies through every part of mind and body, affecting each tiny cell. A new cleavage has as it were been made and all primal elements in the nature strike a new attitude toward the centre of control.

CHECKING the "vagaries of thought," relaxing the tensions of the body, breathing deeply of God's pure air, ignoring the importance of the Ego, steadily pushing the activity of the whole being in the direction in which one wishes it to move, are rules which when followed closely and when working harmoniously are sufficient to introduce one into a new world; aye, a world so large as compared with the treadmill narrowness of a small life and purposeless thinking that it may well be called a universe. This glorified world awaits him who seeks.

DESPONDENCY is an insult to the Creator. It cripples all the faculties He has given. It should be rooted out of one's nature as any other vice. It should be sublimated into cheer.

THE soul will plod on in certain directions blindly if it must, but when the lamp of intelligence is lighted it walks boldly without wavering or fall.

WE hear about the art of forgetting. It is more than an art. It is a positive essential in one's mental equipment if one would make progress in the spiritual life.

THE art of forgetting one thing is the art of remembering another. The thing which we wish to forget must be supplanted in our minds by the definite thing upon which we wish to concentrate the attention. Thus it happens that the mastery of physical weaknesses and temperamental defects and the gain in mental power are, after all, brought about by cultivation of spiritual qualities. It is only as spiritual qualities, positive and strong, supplant the things in ourselves which we wish to forget that the desideratum is attained, namely, the control of all our forces and the enjoyment of our lives.

THE secret of working easily, without tiring, is an intelligent understanding and adjustment of the mutual relation of spirit, mind, nerve and muscle. These are all separate and distinct things and yet they are one. The body should be in such a position that the life fluids may flow through it without obstruction. No muscles should be taut except those required for the particular work that is being performed. The nerves should be steady, not jumping erratically because of agitation in the mind. The mental powers must be concentrated upon the work in hand, and the soul must be without rebellion.

ONE may travel the world over in *search* of peace and never know it until he *makes* it. Let him make use of the mighty sceptre which God has given him and command the elements at war within his own breast.

THE downpour of water from the skies is essential to the life of the trees. The rain of sorrow in our lives must be drawn into our life-blood, else we too shall wither and perish and fail of the growth we were born to accomplish. Living according to the laws of nature we expand day by day as inevitably and unconsciously as do the trees.

THAT in your temperament which you recognize as your greatest weakness may become not only your greatest strength but the source of your greatest enjoyment, since by means of mastering a weakness you learn the law which brings to you its opposite good.

REAL goodness is not so common a thing in this world. It may even be said to be rare. It is not a subterfuge into which one flees because he lacks ability or will. Rather is it ability and will only which can acquire the actual good.

LAW prevails in the so-called lower as well as the higher. It is for us to choose whether we will live under the preponderating influence of laws which bring about a lesser degree of happiness, or under laws which mould us into creatures of a finer fibre, capable of seeing in our environment that to which we were formerly blind, capable of enjoying that which formerly conveyed no meaning to us.

THE unspeakable relief which comes to a person who struggles with an unhappy temperament when one day he suddenly turns his back upon it all, is only to be understood by those who suffer the miseries of such an existence and into whose hearts at last the floods of spiritual light are poured. The instant the spirit is thus freed, light-heartedness springs into being at a bound, involuntarily, necessarily, for it is the struggle itself which makes the heavy heart. The joy which is the accompaniment of vigorous, energetic action then supplants the heaviness of lackadaisical, paralyzing struggle.

THE Divine Will reveals to its devoted followers more and more of its purport and wisdom. Follow not the Will and you may become blind.

NO one should feel that because he is locked in his own chamber for the hour he may give free play to unworthy thought and ignoble feeling, he may safely indulge in melancholy or despair. This does not mean that he may not occasionally be "off guard," as it were. If it did, privacy would contribute little toward the recuperation of our powers. But when alone one may entertain the angel of his better self even more charmingly perhaps than when in the presence of others.

LIFE may be glorious every day. The spirit may wrap itself round in cloud-like airiness, so light, so beautiful, so penetrating, that all which is ugly is softened by it and disappears from our view.

THE healthful discipline that comes from daily work when one takes pleasure in it is valuable beyond computation. The power to direct the mental faculties undisturbed by the turmoil of surroundings is of the greatest imaginable good, and this power acquired in daily discipline will be of service wherever one goes. The contact with our kind in general, high and low, superiors and inferiors, refined and coarse, brings to the surface the shining beauty of true character, as stones rubbed together only polish and make brighter the beauty of the priceless gem. Why then need the worker complain of his lot? Rather let him glory in it. Daily work is many a soul's salvation. Daily work *may* grow for us wings instead of forging for us fetters.

"ABATEMENT of thought" expresses tersely a mental process which should be within the power of all. Rather, it expresses an action of the spirit upon the mind, causing it to refrain from working at will. No one who has not acquired the ability to abate the thought to a greater or lesser degree knows the highest spiritual peace which he is capable of attaining. It may be that the thought can never wholly cease while life lasts, as the body may not stop its breathing. But surely it is that when riotous thought abates, peace and joy roll over the kingdom. I remember the beautiful words of P. Rámanáthan — I do not know whether he himself was quoting — that "Thoughts are the warp and woof of the veil which hides from us the face of God. Lift the veil and God is there."

HAPPINESS

Knew'st thou the truth, thou wouldst not pray:
Lord to thy child send joy this day.
Thou art deceived: joy is within,
And never pain nor grief nor sin
Can take't away. God put it there.
Nor comes it nearer thee for prayer.
Joy is of thy true self a part —
Why shouldst thou pray for what thou art?

— MARY PUTNAM GILMORE.

The full throat of the world is charged with song,
Morning and twilight melt with ecstasy
In the high heat of noon. Simply to be,
Palpitant where the green spring forces·throng,
Eager for life, life unashamed and strong —
This is desire fulfilled. Exalted, free,
The spirit gains her ether, scornfully
Denies existence that is dark or wrong.

This is enough, to see the song begun
Which shall be finished in some field afar.
Laugh that the night may still contain a star,
Nor idly moan your impotence of grace.
Life is a song, lift up your care-free face
Gladly and gratefully toward the sun.

— HELEN HAY WHITNEY.

HAPPINESS

LET us learn to dwell in the upper chambers of our being. There the mental atmosphere is always clear, the moral horizon is unflecked by clouds, only enchanting distance and mysterious space meet the gaze of the Ego through the windows of the purified soul.

TO be keenly sensitive to the ugly and the bad is to be delicately sensitive to the beautiful and the good. To be sufferingly sensitive to human inharmonies is to be joyfully alive to enlightened lawfulness. So closely akin are joy and sorrow that while one hand may be pressing a heavy heart, the other may be stretching upward toward the stars.

WHEN one comes into virtual possession of the wealth of the universe through conscious affinity with it, poverty in material things is no longer to be feared. Who can rob us of the soil over which we lightly tread? Who can deprive us of the air we freely and deeply breathe? Who can bar from our vision the beauty of sky and star? Who can alter by one slightest shade the glorious coloring of the landscape or the gorgeousness of the setting sun?

WE wish for freedom to live, to act, *within* the perfect laws of God, yet independent of the laws of man, which must be ever changing, never perfect. This does not mean law*less*ness, but law*ful*ness. Man's laws are only an approach to those of nature, an imperfect copy of them. He who sees nature's law back of man-made law will not disobey the latter and it will be no bondage to him. His own natural law is the higher.

ONE touch of real sorrow is worth a thousand days of that which is ordinarily considered happiness unalloyed. And what is sorrow but contact with the realities of life, with the seriousness of death, with the wonders of God's ways? Why should we then wish that sorrow never enter our path? Sorrow? It is not sorrow,— that is only our name for it. It is the opening of the clouds before us, giving us a glimpse of the vastness of Heaven. It is God's hand appearing out of the haze pointing to a glory never yet conceived in our days of simple, complacent happiness.

IN the course of time all Nature assumes for us a character of intelligence, of life, and her laws become friendly creatures. We may commune with them, yield to them, trust them, feel ourselves shielded and protected by them.

Even the darkness of the night is friendly. It hushes us to repose, it soothes us to sleep. Why need one be restlessly wakeful when thus closely befriended? The space and the silence are full of stirring creatures, our many friends.

ILLUMINATION from within transfigures all upon which it falls. Thus again may we make a new world about us. It is the nature of light to transfigure and the object seen takes on a special hue from the character of the light which shines upon it.

FATE is my mission, my loved work, the particular work which I can do better than I can do other things, the work which I can do better than some one else can do it. Fate is a mighty friend in disguise.

LET no one say that he cannot live a successful, happy life in the spot where his birth places him or in places where the trend of events takes him. The inner life, the life of strength, nobility, patience, effort, dignity, beauty, depends not upon its location in the material world, depends not on outer surroundings, but rather by its own inherent force does it draw unto itself from earth and heaven the strong vital currents which mingling make for that life a new atmosphere, make for that life almost a new environment. So translucent in time may that atmosphere become that the soul, without moving the body from one spot, may have a vision far exceeding in acuteness and range the vision of the insatiate traveler, though his travels be world-wide.

PRIDE of attainment in spiritual things is inconsistent with that attainment. Rather should we be grateful that we have been brought under the law.

WHY not repose in the protecting goodness of the Powers that Be? Surely it cannot be that the Maker of majestic orbs travelling nightly their course across the heavens, suggesting to us unerring law and flashing down upon us their starry brilliancy, will leave His human children uncared for and adrift.

A BLOW like death knocks us out of our petty selves.

THE mercurial temperament suffers more than the phlegmatic. It must be remembered, however, that the mercurial temperament senses various degrees of heat and cold in its atmospheric environment, and when Mercury cultivates his intellect he is able to pick and choose the climate in which he shall daily dwell.

IT is a blessed thing to give of our substance and feel it no denial, not because we have much, but because we wish to give that which we have.

LIFE is serious, or should be. Yet it is the man who is apparently the most serious who most easily bursts into the happy laughter of the light of heart. The deeply serious man looks into the principles of being, into the laws of life, understands the secrets of the Most High. He is the man then who may at times be lifted into the bright airiness of God's fairy lands.

WE find ourselves at times in states of mind which seem to be those of transition. We do not quite understand what is taking place within. Things that once would have given us pleasure have lost their attraction. Occurrences which once would have caused in us excessive emotion no longer have that power. Affection itself seems to wane and dependence on our friends is less binding. We are a little fearful lest in some way past our comprehension and beyond our control our hold on life is weakening and our interest flagging. Yet we need not be anxious. Transition states such as these are glorious harbingers of better things to come. Irksome bondage of the flesh is dropping off and freedom is being acquired. Let us welcome always the advance, be watchful, trustful and calm. The resistless laws of nature are sweeping us on.

DEATH saddens? It must be sweet to lay down the burdens of life and fall asleep in the arms of God, just as we lay down the burdens of a day and fall asleep in the arms of night. And as God speaks to us in the darkness of the night, bidding us lay down the burdens of the day, so he calls us by the cloudiness of death to lay down the burdens of life. Let us reverence and welcome both the darkness of night and the cloudiness of death, for God is in both.

ONE is always happy in conscious power when exerted for good. Spirit unhampered is strong. Therefore by as much as we free the spirit, give play and exercise to its attributes, by so much do we become consciously powerful, by so much do we grow like unto the gods.

LET us cling to a friendship which shows itself persisting through differences of opinion, divergence of interests and separation of lives. Such a friendship proves that the heart is stronger than the head and that the heart's needs are all-important.

IF one listen, listen, with concentrated spirit-attention, just as he would listen with the physical ear were he trying to catch a sound, he will hear many beautiful things which pass unheeded by the busybody and the listless.

RENEWED consecration to holiness of life and nobility of conduct will always and immediately lift one from the slough of despond.

WHEREIN is depth different from height? Well may he who can look into the depths of the Commonplace and wrest from it its meaning be envied by his fellow-man and not despised by him who is on the mountain top. Delicate courtesy compels us and the commonest relations in life never cease to be objects of beauty when we see them as the marvels that they are.

THE term that we glibly use, "Face of Nature," is itself suggestive of life, for in a human face there is the expression of all the qualities that make up the soul. Let us call it then face of nature, or face of God. If we are akin with it, it will be very much alive. Then we shall see in the changing clouds, the waving trees, the widest waters, only the expression of the unseen life aback, responsive to each sentiment of our own, answering each appeal. We do not need the language of words when love shines upon us from a beaming countenance. Then why are we so deaf to this most eloquent message that comes to us from the face of Nature, revealing the Almighty Soul behind?

INEXPRESSIBLE is the joy of having found a confidence that replaces fear, a trust that takes the place of doubt, a composure wrought out of agitation, light that banishes darkness, and a freedom that breaks down all prison walls.

VARIOUS INTIMATIONS

It is a mystery of the unknown
  That fascinates us; we are children still,
  Wayward and wistful; with one hand we cling
To the familiar things we call our own,
  And with the other, resolute of will,
Grope in the dark for what the day will bring.

— Henry Wadsworth Longfellow.

Prais'd be the fathomless universe,
For life and joy, and for objects and knowledge curious,
And for love, sweet love — but praise! praise! praise!
For the sure-enwinding arms of cool-enfolding death.

— Walt Whitman.

'By her own strength can Virtue live?
  Self-poised can Hope wide-winging soar?'
List! for our deepening age shall give
  Some answer surer than of yore; —
Stand fast, high hearts, thro' woe and weal;
  Watch thro' the night, if watch ye may;
Wait, till the rifted heavens reveal
  Unheard-of morning, mystic day.

— F. W. H. Myers.

VARIOUS INTIMATIONS

BLESSED is the man for whom the mystery of life has become a continual attraction, who sees beauty mirrored in its depths, and a divine significance to it all.

ASTRONOMERS are endeavoring to discover the nature of life on the planet Mars. Yet what has that life to do with us? If it were not that our globe itself is unfolding, giving forth its secrets to the questioning mind of man; if it were not that the race as a race is evolving, acquiring new powers with each passing generation, there might be some reason in the claim that what the Creator has not seen fit to reveal to us He never intended we should know. Yet it is not at all inconceivable that with newly evolved powers of the human mind, with ever higher attainment in spiritual living, with more finely attenuated human organisms, means will be found in the not distant future by which we may even become cognizant of the interests of our neighbors on the ruddy orb which we name Mars. If friends who have passed from our sight are living on still, they must be not only in some place but in a state of real vitality. Can it be wrong to try to reach them?

CONCENTRATION is the withdrawing of the mind from the many to the few, from the multitudinous to the homogeneous, from complexity to simplicity, from manifestation to the unmanifest, from the material to the spiritual, from the agitated to the calm. If one wishes one may find sleep through concentration,— sleep, the withdrawal of the Ego from the outer to the inner, from the seen to the unseen.

WHEN I was a child I looked at the pale green of the western sky, tinged here and there with rose, and something within me responded to this beauty which I beheld at a distance. It stirrd within me an unutterable longing to be able to express in my own nature a purity such as I saw emblazoned there. Surely God's handiwork appeals to the inner eye, the organ of the inmost self.

MY real life, that which I feel surging through my body, welling up in my emotions and bursting out from my brain, is independent of time and space every day. Death then only marks the end of *certain* actions and a *certain* course of conduct, as the hour of dusk marks off the actions of the day.

DIGNITY is more becoming than self-consciousness. Dignity is self-consciousness grown divine.

THIS straining after arguments to prove that the Ego survives the death of the body seems needless, seems at times folly to the soul that is conscious that wherever it moves it walks among *living* things, that nowhere is there *really* death, but only transformation.

I *CRAVE* that which satisfies my ideal of spiritual dignity and beauty, as one looks constantly in the material for beauty of form and color.

THE glow that one feels from closeness to the Great Impersonal may be just as vivid as that which flows from bodily contact with a human friend,—nay, more so. The human soul can touch the Eternal, and the human soul when linked with the Over-Soul generates new and wonderful powers.

GENTLENESS in the human countenance is more beautiful than assertion. The mild eye is more pleasing than the sharp, and may sparkle with a lovelier light. The saintly man appears to breathe out gentleness from every portion of his body.

THE EGO has many kith and kin in the Universe whom it may take delight in meeting when the sheath of the personality is laid aside.

LOVE and selflessness make the vision clear.

IT is true that there are, here and there in our very midst, individuals who claim to be repositories of what is known as "Hermetic Philosophy," the knowledge of which is not to be found in printed books but has been handed down by sure means from the wisdom of the past. It is well known that many truths relating to the material universe, only recently established by science, were known to Eastern sages many years ago, secrets of the Cosmos wrung from it by I know not what sort of spiritual acumen. This occult lore is so vast in its scope that it comprehends as a matter of course life on more planes than one, and, among its privileged initiates, to speak of death as ending all seems an affront to their intelligence as well as to their faith. Notwithstanding this, the masses, the millions, bury in the black earth the dear bodies of their friends and turn away with that terrible sinking of the heart which means that joy has gone out of their lives. They are only conscious that the monster Fate, to which all men must bow, has at last overtaken them. Into such hearts one who sees the light ahead longs to shed a ray of hope.

NEITHER the mind nor the body can be composed if there is agitation at the centre. And calmness is not dullness, it is not inactivity. It is power exerted, it is control of forces, it is intense mental action, it is spiritual energy.

WHEN death comes to one of two who have been inseparable in the bonds of love, one is born into new life on the other side of the Veil, one is born into new life on this side. They go on together as before, except that the thin partition between the Seen and the Unseen divides their bodies but not their souls. Nay, the bond that bound them becomes the sweeter and the stronger. With the great event called death between them, both open new eyes to God's wonders at one and the same time. "The flesh does not conjoin, but dissever; although through its very severance it suggests a shadow of the union which it cannot bestow." [1]

IT will give us delight to trust the goodness of the Universe, aye its friendliness, as if it were a personal being. These impersonal qualities may become real to us, as though embodied in human form, and our confidence in them increase.

[1] F. W. H. Myers, Human Personality, Vol. I, p. 112.

NO one is great who cannot sacrifice himself whenever and wherever he is actually called upon to do so. Needless self-sacrifice is a degradation to the soul.

WE love people who are imperfect. We love people who are less perfect than ourselves. Let us do what we can by word or deed or silent force to bring our loved ones up, but let us never sink to their level if it be below our own, however much we love them.

IN brief moments of unconsciousness or in longer hours of absorption, time for us is not. It appears, then, that there is no such thing as time, but only occurrences in consciousness. Yet when we recall a definite epoch from out the dimness of the past, time stretches out at length. Why? Because we ourselves have walked on apace, because much has transpired within.

TO the finely developed mind of the naturally sensitive person it must be only the thinnest of veils that separates him from the denizens of another and higher world, for he himself draws his breath in those elements which apparently are the sustainers of life in that higher world.

WHEN I was a child I conceived of the soul as a mass of white or pearly mist, oval in form, located somewhere in the trunk of the body. Now I sometimes picture the spiritual body as an expansion of something far more delicate than mist; not confined to the trunk of the body but permeating and radiating from it; not white or pearly but aglow with delicate and various colors, approaching to whiteness in proportion as the Ego is pure; with centres of thought or light scattered through it like nuclei; keeping in general the bodily form yet shooting from these nuclei its search-light rays, which pierce more deeply into the abyss of the Unknown according as the soul is great.

THERE is a dignity of spiritual consciousness and a dignified way of living which is not obliged to be constantly asking itself how it shall dress, how it shall act, how it shall talk. All these minor things fall into harmonious relation with the superior creature within who has accomplished this feat of dignified living. Great dignity of character makes one ashamed to ask how its possessor is garbed, in fact almost blinds altogether to the fact that he is garbed at all. Yet if we take note of particulars it will be apparent that the garment is becoming and fitting. Some subtle essence emanates from the cultured soul, blending the outer apparel into the harmony of the whole.

THERE are more things in the possibilities of the seeker than are dreamt of in the philosophy of the dogmatist.

IT may do injury to those who have passed away to wish them to keep in touch with the sorrows of this life, but it cannot injure them to keep in touch with its loves. Selfish grief on our part may hold them back in their career, but true love in this world or any other can do naught but bless. Love loves the lovely, and love itself, long-suffering though it be, may at last grow cold if the object that once attracted it be constantly bathed in grief. I think we may judge of them as we judge of ourselves, when we ask the question, is it wrong to expect them to keep in touch with our lives.

ONE who learns the art of living easily here is becoming fitted to enter naturally into life beyond. It is *only* spiritual living that is easy. What conception can the mole have of the glory of the sunlit heavens? Yet the robin perches on the swaying bough, the lark soars upward toward the blue, and the eagle ranges the mountain top. When we look into the earth, blackness bars our vision. When we look into the heavens there is no limit to the glory, save the weakness in the physical eye.

THE more devotedly one loves a single person the more is his heart open to lesser degrees of friendly relation.

IT would seem that each grade of matter were permeable by a finer which is its life, and that when the finer is withdrawn from the coarser the latter dies. In relation to our coarser bodies the air is spirit, is the breath of life. It is not at all difficult to conceive, analogously, of those we call dead inhabiting a finer than fleshly form, which must in the nature of things be invisible to our outward sense, even as is pure air.

THE simple, devoted soul has faith; the intelligent, knowing soul has a greater. Trust may be the accompaniment of ignorance; a greater trust is the accompaniment of wisdom.

THE newly bereaved stands mourner beside the open grave. The deathly stillness that prevails but faintly symbolizes the deadly inaction of his heart. Man tries in myriad ways to keep before his eyes in enduring bronze and marble a reminder of death. Yet above all these silent testimonials waves the green of the foliage and shines the blue of the ether, both palpitating with life. Let the mourner but look upward, and with steady gaze the heart gradually succumbs to nature's persuasion, and the bronze and the marble lose their terror.

GOD speaks to us in flower and star and sky, in love and tenderness and suffering. The word " language " means that which can be uttered by the tongue, but many thousand things are communicated to us by other means. Let us call it speaking, for lack of a more accurate term. Can you hear the speech which God utters every hour in every place? A speech more eloquent than language, as the speech of the eye is more eloquent than the uttered word. God speaks through the perfection of human beauty in another, through grace, through composure of soul. These are about us every day. Let us listen for the music of their voice.

AFTER disillusionment life becomes increasingly wonderful, interesting and inviting. Not the outer world of sense, but the inner meanings of things; the tremendous significance of it all and its fathomless depths. These are the things that now attract.

IF a deep love for one person possess our heart, it should, while losing none of its individual strength, be gradually sublimated into the impersonal quality, like unto that which exists in the bosom of the Infinite.

IT has ever been one of the mysteries of life that we must give up in order to own, that we must sacrifice in order to possess, that we must die daily to ourselves in order to realize the *larger* self. A kind deed by the wayside, then, has a far deeper significance than the mere earning of a little happiness as we pass. It is a part of the complicated network of relationship that binds all human beings together and bears us all onward toward the possession of better life. It is, in the language of a Myers, "that universal scheme by which the higher helps the lower, and the stronger the weaker, through all the ideal relationships of the world of life."

WE say that the spirit is a spark from God, but from birth onward it must be constantly fanned into greater glow until its scintillation becomes a light divine.

WITH a person who is conscious of universal life, to whom the distant star and the whole starry host seem friendly, it is wholly contrary to what has become his normal thought to relegate to the category of the dead an intelligent loved or an intense lover. The harmony of the plane on which such a person habitually dwells would be destroyed by non-belief.

THE mystic seeks God in every department of life. To be a mystic is not necessarily to be a recluse.

LET it be remembered that there are persons who are finer built, more delicately sensitive, more spiritually sublimated than are we ourselves. And it behooves us to listen with respect when they tell us of existence in higher conditions and on planes of finer matter than we ourselves know.

THE spiritual life, what is it, either here or there? The person who strives daily to live as much of that life as is possible to *him*, the best that is revealed to *his* understanding, comes in time to realize strength, vitality, goodness, joyousness, all things satisfying in themselves, to such degree that his questions are all answered in himself. This new strong unfoldment within himself, this thing that he perceives grows larger daily, *is* life itself, and to call *life death* is an absurdity.

LET us invent a new term for the taking leave of the body by the spirit. Let it be one to which no faint touch of sadness clings. The mystery and the loveliness in death overshadow its sadness.

UNTIL we know what death is, we do not know what life is; until we know what loss is, we do not know what love is.

LOVE

Comfort our souls with love,—
Love of all human kind;
Love special, close — in which, like sheltered dove,
Each weary heart its own safe nest may find;
And love that turns above
Adoringly, contented to resign
All loves, if need be, for the Love Divine.

— Dinah Mulock Craik.

LOVE

LOVE is too lofty a theme to be broached by any but the wisest minds, to be handled by any but reverent hands. From the view-point of this chapter I may but look at it from afar, may but kiss the hem of its garment; yet with that touch and that look know that its effulgence is spread over me, that its virtue passes through me.

LOVE unlocks closed portals, builds a beautiful archway through the densest of woods.

LOVE is a pain, an aching, yet sings when all else is sad.

THE death of the loved one brings life to the lover.

LOVE looks out through open windows, lays a hand on the departing soul.

LOVE blinds because it dazzles.

LOVE envelops one in a beautiful soft mist which sheds its whiteness on all around. It must then be of the nature of ethereal light.

LOVE pierces the farthest vistas, knows that sometime, somewhere, it may claim its own.

LOVE purified, intensified, floods the heart with light and wisdom.

LOVE loses its loveliness in too many words.

www.ingramcontent.com/pod-product-compliance
Lightning Source LLC
Chambersburg PA
CBHW020643230426
43665CB00008B/299

* 9 7 8 1 4 4 5 5 4 3 0 7 9 *